# "A NEWFOUNDLAND SON"

## AUTOBIOGRAPHY

Nathan Budgell, DVM

COPYRIGHT © 2000, 2001 BY NATHAN MCKINLEY BUDGELL
All rights reserved.
No part of this book may be reproduced, restored in a retrieval system, or transmitted by means, electronic, mechanical, photocopying, recording, or otherwise, without written consent from the author.

ISBN: 0-75961-448-2

This book is printed on acid free paper.

1stBooks - rev. 3/8/01

## ACKNOWLEDGEMENTS

My thanks go first to my wife and constant loving companion, Sharrie, for her unwavering support thro' my life and also her grammatical know-how towards this book.

Next to thank are my five children, Peter, Ralph, Libby, Daphne and David, for their patience, understanding and love.

Also to two of our dear friends of some sixty years, who were accomplices during our courtship, Gord and Willie (Wilson) Jinks, who sequestered the engagement ring during three turbulent years.

Marianne (Royds) Lynch, recently deceased, who was with us when I proposed marriage.

Doreen Doth, who did her best to put my book together.

Photo credits to The International Grenfell Association of St. Anthony, Newfoundland.

Lastly, but not least, many thanks to my son Ralph and his wife Leigh who did the final edits and layout.

Toiling, rejoicing, sorrowing onward through life he goes,
Each morning sees some task begun,
Each evening sees it close.
Something attempted, something done,
Has earned a night's repose.

                                                Oliver Goldsmith


As water flows, its steady drift upon the land so lean,
As sunlight filters through the air,
Its radiance seldom seen.
As drifting clouds form through the sky,
Making new-borne strife,
As generations come and go,
Producing drift of life.

                                                Ralph Budgell

# TABLE OF CONTENTS

CHAPTER I - THE BEGINNINGS ..................................................................... 1

CHAPTER II - THE ORPHANAGE ..................................................................... 7

CHAPTER III - SIR WILFRED GRENFELL ..................................................... 22

CHAPTER IV - MY BENEFACTRESS - CHRISTINE FELLOWS ................... 27

CHAPTER V - ENGLAND .................................................................................. 34

CHAPTER VI - BACK HOME ............................................................................ 51

CHAPTER VII - NORTH WEST RIVER ........................................................... 57

CHAPTER VIII - TRAPPING IN LABRADOR ................................................. 63

CHAPTER IX - THE DEPRESSION YEARS ..................................................... 88

CHAPTER X - UNIVERSITY .............................................................................. 94

CHAPTER XI - ENGLAND AGAIN ................................................................... 99

CHAPTER XII - AFTER GRADUATION ......................................................... 102

CHAPTER XIII - COURTSHIP .......................................................................... 106

CHAPTER XIV - BACK TO NEWFOUNDLAND ........................................... 113

CHAPTER XV - NIAGARA FALLS .................................................................. 120

CHAPTER XVI - HAMMOND FARM .............................................................. 123

CHAPTER XVII - WHALING ............................................................................ 137

CHAPTER XVIII - THE SEAL HUNT .............................................................. 147

CHAPTER XIX - MIGUASHA LODGE ............................................................ 151

CHAPTER XX - RETIREMENT ........................................................................ 155

# PROLOGUE

Writing one's memoirs, I am constantly reminded of the fact that the only thing one can take off the stage, which he did not bring into it, is the record of a sojourn through life. Many writers would dearly like to revise the record of their early days but these have to stand. Suffice it to say, however, that my forebears immigrated to Newfoundland in June 1774 from the West Country of England. One branch of the family came from Fowey in Dorsetshire, the other from Great Yarmouth. They were all engaged in fishing, which before the advent of the modern rapacious methods later dominating the fish harvest, provided a simple yet lucrative living for the many families which populated the coastal villages of England. The Elizabethan dialect spoken by these people can still be heard in the settlements and outports of Newfoundland. Most of the people who emigrated to the island settled on either the south or east coast, where they would have access to the rich cod fishing areas off the Grand Banks of Newfoundland and Labrador. In addition, the taking of seals coming in the spring on immense ice floes and icebergs provided a welcome supplement to a long winter of salt meat. The seal blubber was used when oil was extracted for lighting and lubricating, while the meat being very nutritious, was also used as dog food. Seals were commonly referred to as swiles. The difficulty in finding medical services located in St. John's, the capital city, some two hundred miles to the south, brought the emigrants to relocate in White Bay where wood, game and fish were plentiful.

Ambrose Langford, third generation son of Enos, one of the original settlers, made several fishing trips to the north of TwillingGate in the area of White Bay, a deep water and sheltered inlet running some eighty kilometers inland from the Atlantic Ocean, practically bisecting the island. Many small coves and safe anchorages existed along its shores where permanent habitation could be had for the taking. Once removed from the cold north-easterlies, the surrounding land seemed like a veritable Garden of Eden.

Henry Langford, a descendant of one of the original settlers, established a sawmill in Brown's Cove, about eight miles from Hampden. Other members of the family married and moved to Sop's Arm, a fishing community about fifteen miles north.

Mother, Henry's sister, occupied a small four-room log cabin, endured many hardships with the severe winter weather. Water was fetched in a barrel from a brook nearby. It was kept in the porch and would invariably freeze at night having to be constantly broken each morning. Wood was furnished from the slab pile produced from the logs being made into saleable lumber. In the fall, the harvest of dry cod was sold to the local merchant who, in turn, shipped it to St.

John's and from there to many countries including Spain, Portugal, Italy and islands of the Caribbean, the chief ones being Jamaica and Barbados.

Berries grew in profusion and were known by such names as the Bay Capple, Cappleberry, or to the native people - Bakeapple. It was not unusual to find the latter prominently displayed on the menu of the Newfoundland Railway or coastal steamers in the dessert section; diners being quite perplexed when the waiter appeared with a dish of yellow berries, instead of a real baked apple. Others such as cranberries were preserved for winter. Red berries could be put in a tub of water and preserved all winter by freezing, remaining fresh with a good texture, even after thawing in the spring.

Mattresses and pillows were filled with down from the ducks and patchwork quilting provided the accessories. Kerosene lamps were used for illumination. Water often had to be hauled by dog team on a sled or "komatik" in empty barrels originally used for salt beef.

During the summer, the weekly coastal steamer brought food staples such as flour by the barrel, sugar, tea, and of course molasses, which came back together with excellent rum from Barbados said to be used as ballast. Molasses with tea, not sugar, was the vogue. It could be readily seen that with a little ingenuity, life in these outports of civilization could be made tolerable. Education, as we view it today, was considered unnecessary, as hard work requiring only physical effort provided the amenities of life.

# CHAPTER I - THE BEGINNINGS

Two of the aunts attending my birth were as different as night and day. Aunt Fanny, the youngest, abhorred the thought of ever having to dress up in anything other than working clothes. She could cuss like a trooper, but to us it was certainly inoffensive. Mother used to say it came "natural like"; that the good Lord was listening all the time and she would be judged some day. Aunt Fanny was the kindest person, however, and could be counted on to help any time of the day or night, anyone in trouble. She was a real "diamond in the rough."

Aunt Joanna, on the other hand, was fastidious in her dress invariably wearing a long black dress trimmed with lace whenever she ventured out of doors. Her words were well chosen, never out of place, the epitome of good breeding.

Aunt Lucy was very ordinary and quietly went about her business. They, together with three brothers, had emigrated from Great Yarmouth in Suffolk, England as young children.

Henry and Rupert Langford, the two eldest, operated the lumber mill. Joseph, the youngest, served in the Royal Newfoundland Regiment during World War I, thereafter leaving for California. He was a self-educated man investing in real estate at Long Beach and Santa Monica, California, becoming very wealthy.

Mother, having a natural aptitude for nursing, acted as mid-wife for some forty-five years in Springdale where we subsequently moved. She often boasted of having "barned" over four hundred babies. I well remember in later years seeing her set out with scissors, tape and clean gauze to deliver a child, mentioning on return, that she had to brew some juniper tea to give strength to the mother. Aunt Susan, as mother was fondly known, was a veritable angel in disguise, to people in an area where doctors or nurses were almost unheard of.

Mother would always venture to Hampton or Brown's Cove to visit "her people", as she would say, her sisters and brothers. My only remaining first cousin Jane Naccarri resides in Seattle, Washington. In 1997, we had the pleasure of visiting with her in Seattle. As well, she traveled with us to British Columbia and Alberta for a visit with our son Ralph and his family.

**Figure 1 Sarah Jane (Langford) Naccarri and Sharrie, my wife - 1996.**

Lumber prices fell off during the summer of 1911 so my father decided to move to Springdale, in Hall's Bay, about 130 miles, by sea, from Brown's Cove. He was offered work by the firm of Warr Brothers who had contracted to cut wood for the paper mill in Grand Falls and lumber for the sawmill in Springdale. The firm owned a large general store, supplying fishing gear to the town's people who, enjoying the fruits of a lucrative herring fishery, also arranged to market their catch abroad. Payment was rarely made in the form of cash, but rather in vouchers on the store for needed supplies. This practice was also extended to the woodsmen, and it seemed that they never appeared to get out of debt to the merchant. The deep waters of Hall's Bay allowed ocean-going ships to penetrate several miles inland to load wood and hundreds of barrels of herring.

Father acquired a piece of land some ten acres in area under a grant in the name of King George V, and proceeded to build a frame house. Mother, in the meantime, had to fend for all of the family of five. She, in subsequent years, told me of having to hunt, fish, cut wood, carry water and scrub our linen in a tub using an old-fashioned washboard. On one occasion she provided fresh caribou meat by chasing one of the animals into the water and hitting it over the head with a paddle. Bedtime came when darkness fell as she could ill afford to buy very much kerosene to fuel the lamps.

Figure 2 Lucy Blachlar (Cousin), Grace (6), George (2), Nathan (4 mos), Susan (my mother), Peter (8) and Bertha (10).

Finally, in the summer of 1914, the house in Springdale was finished and mother loaded the five of us, and a few belongings, into a small, fourteen-foot rowboat. We headed for Springdale, a distance of some 135 miles, stopping off at small fishing communities along the way for food and shelter. In this modern age it may seem inconceivable to think of anyone, particularly a woman, undertaking a journey of this magnitude. The little craft was exposed to the full fury of the Atlantic Ocean from a point called Fleur de Lys to La Scie, a distance of thirty miles. However, at La Scie, a kind relative put us all in his motor boat and towed our frail boat around treacherous Cape St. John and into the calmer waters of Notre Dame Bay, putting us ashore at Tilt Cove on the tip of the Bay Verte peninsula. We stayed there four days and I was told we completed the remainder of the journey in easy stages, arriving at Springdale several days later. The trip took a little over six weeks to complete.

It seemed that at last Dame Fortune had smiled upon us. Father had a steady job as a woodsman in winter while working at the sawmill in summer. He continued to improve the house in his spare time and mother concentrated on her garden, in addition to building up a flock of fifteen sheep, four goats and a few hens. She also planted plum and apple trees, many varieties of berry bushes and grew excellent vegetables. This, in conjunction with her midwifery skills, provided substance for a growing family.

**Figure 3 My Father – Peter Budgell.**

Father, accompanied by the older children, would catch codfish in the cold deep waters of Hall's Bay. This was not looked upon as a chore, but rather a sport. A "Jigger" in the shape of a lead herring with two hooks protruding from its mouth was lowered over the side of the boat until it hit bottom. It was then raised about six feet to attract cod usually feeding at that depth. The jigging action began by pulling up and down on the line attracting and hooking the fish that were quite numerous. Often three to four dozen were caught in one evening, then split and salted for winter use.

As is often the case with life that when it seems brightest, fate can deal a cruel blow. Father, while working in the woods in the late fall of 1914, contracted pneumonia. He returned home, and in spite of all the care a loving wife could give, died in the spring of 1915. By this time, my youngest sister Eva was born, thus leaving mother with six children, all under the age of twelve. With a meager widow's pension of six dollars a month, it was impossible to make ends meet. Only through the generosity of the people of Springdale, were we able to survive. My eldest sister, Bertha, was sent out into service as a housemaid and the second, namely Grace, scrubbed floors for a mere pittance when not in school. My eldest brother, Peter, though not yet nine, assumed the role of "father" carrying water from a nearby brook, cutting wood and generally helping with house chores. George, baby Eva and I needed constant attention.

Six months after father's death, and out of desperation, mother married John Critch, a fisherman. He was subject to frequent fits of temper, often manifesting into physical abuse.

In the fall of 1915, the Grenfell Hospital ship, "Strathcona," came into Springdale on a routine trip. It had been dispensing medical services to fishermen along the coast from St. Anthony, headquarters of the Grenfell Mission to Deep-Sea Fishermen. The plight of our family, plus the Critch's, was brought to the attention of the medical officer in charge. He suggested taking some of us to the orphanage in St. Anthony, where we would be well cared for and sent to school. Thus it was that Peter, George and I arrived in St. Anthony in late September 1915. John Critch decided to keep Bertha and Grace who, although young children, were potential money earners. Eva was of course too young to leave and I have since thanked my lucky stars that I was not old enough to remember the pangs and grief of being separated from my family. I would not see them again for many years. It has always been beyond my comprehension, and that of my older siblings, why it was not agreed, since times were so tough, to send two of Critch's children along with two of ours to the orphanage, rather than mother's three young boys.

## CHAPTER II - THE ORPHANAGE

The Grenfell Mission at St. Anthony was founded by Sir Wilfred Grenfell, who was later Knighted by King George V. He was an English doctor born in 1865 at Parkgate, Cheshire. Later he attended a London Hospital and then university. It was in his second year there that he dedicated his life to Christ at a tent meeting in Shadwell. The famous evangelistic team of Moody and Sankey conducted the service. He studied medicine under the great Sir Frederick Treeves, and upon graduating, became a member of the College of Physicians and Surgeons. After serving as medical officer among the fishermen on the Dogger Banks in the North Sea, under the auspices of the Royal National Mission to Deep Sea Fishermen, a new and challenging opportunity came.

Lord Southborough, having just returned from Newfoundland in 1891, spoke of the need for assistance to the fishermen of the North West Atlantic, some twenty thousand of whom conducted a thriving fishery in the waters of Labrador and Newfoundland each year. Accidents and sickness were rife but no medical assistance was at any time available. Grenfell was intensely interested, and because of his previous experience on the Dogger Banks, was selected to go and make a complete survey. This, however, was not until he had firmly decided that it was his Christian duty.

**Figure 4 St.Anthony's Wharf – Hospital ship is on the left.**

He set sail in a small ketch rigged ship named the Albert, from Great Yarmouth in the spring of 1892. After a voyage of seventeen days, a high evergreen-crowned coastline greeted his eyes, just a little north of the Harbour of St. John's, Capital of Newfoundland. As he approached the harbour, the offshore wind grew hotter and hotter and on entering, saw that the whole city was in flames for the third time in its history. Notwithstanding, it was arranged that Dr. Grenfell accompany the large fleet of fishing vessels preparing to embark on their annual voyage to the Labrador fishery.

After some weeks, during which he visited many of the fishing outports and permanent settlements, he realized quite obviously that something would have to be done. Diseases such a beriberi, scurvy and tuberculosis were wide spread, and serious accidents were common among the fishermen. Returning to St. John's, he tried to arouse interest in the immediate problems. He returned to England in October and made a detailed report to the Council of the Royal National Mission to Deep-Sea Fishermen. It was decided to send the good ship Albert back. In the spring, she set sail again having on board two doctors and two nurses.

During the summer, two cottage hospitals were established, one at Battle Harbour and another at Indian Harbour, both on the Labrador Coast. The large trading firm of Baine Johnson, at the former site, was engaged in supplying the fishing fleet. Their help proved invaluable to the workers at the fledgling nursing stations.

In 1901, a small hospital was opened at St. Anthony on the northern tip of Newfoundland. Because of its sheltered harbour and proximity to the main fishing area, it was decided to make it the permanent headquarters of the Mission. In due course, a modern well-equipped building was erected; in addition an orphanage, school, co-op store, machine shop and farm were completed.

**Figure 5 Grenfell Mission Orphanage**
**Addition on the left side was added in 1916.**

Into the orphanage came three fatherless members of the Budgell family - Peter, George and Nathan. It would be seen that two of us were named after biblical personalities, as was the custom in Newfoundland. Mine, Nathan, was "Gift of God," but I doubt if the then kind superintendent, a Miss Katie Spalding, concurred with this interpretation. She decided the first thing I needed was a good bath, having been on board ship for three days with no bathing facilities. I, of course, strongly objected, but after a lengthy struggle and much screaming, she finally convinced me it was for my own good. For several nights she tucked me in her bed and mothered me until I could adjust to my new environment.

**Figure 6 Orphanage Children and Handicraft Workers – 1920.
I am the boy seated on the right.**

Miss Spalding told me all of this many years later in her London office. She was fulfilling the duties of voluntary head of the Grenfell Association of Great Britain and Ireland. In addition, she served ten years as voluntary head of the orphanage, a task utterly exhausting and demanding, which, only a person with her intelligence and devotion, spiced with a saving sense of humour, could have coped with for so long.

One of my earliest recollections of orphanage life was seeing Santa Claus arrive in a sleigh pulled by real live reindeer. Dr. Grenfell introduced the animals into Newfoundland with the help of the Boston Transcript and the Canadian Department of Agriculture. He felt that since large areas of natural food existed, they would provide a valuable and much needed adjunct to the diet and also supply milk and deer skin for clothing and footwear. Unfortunately, in a few short years, the original herd of fifteen hundred had been reduced to two hundred and fifty through poaching and stray dogs. Grenfell requested the Canadian Government to remove them. They were caught and transported to the island of Anticosti in the Gulf of St. Lawrence. I remember quite vividly a dead reindeer being brought to the village on a sled to be used as evidence against the poachers. Grenfell was empowered to act as magistrate and showed little mercy in these cases.

Figure 7 View of St. Anthony in the summer, late 1920's.

The orphanage, as were all the other buildings, was made of wood with accommodation for thirty to fifty children. Many of them were not actually orphaned, but lived in areas so remote that it was felt advisable to bring them to a center where schooling was available. The administrative help was voluntary and recruited from many countries. This made the mission international in its truest sense and, at the same time, interdenominational while carrying on in undenominational work. Viewed in this light, it could be described as an effort, voluntary in its essence by persons motivated by real Christianity. Dr. Grenfell was anxious, and even insisted, that this spirit of cooperation and zeal be evident in the everyday routine of all involved. Prayer meetings each evening and on Sundays, in the absence of a minister, were held exhorting workers to follow in the steps of the Master.

Following Miss Spalding's years of service, several other "Mistresses" came to the orphanage. It was also decided to engage men to supervise the boys who were reaching an age when they probably resented the authority of women.

The first to come was a Mr. Clagett who, unfortunately, was not very experienced in guiding red-blooded youngsters and so left after a short while. Eddie Goodale who was later on to accompany Admiral Richard Byrd on his first South Pole expedition as a dog team driver superseded him. He took an intense interest in us and was well liked. He would take us on expeditions into the surrounding woods teaching us how to use an axe, and at the same time, explaining and identifying tree and moss varieties. Occasionally, we would take along fishing rods, mostly home-made and catch a mess of brook trout which were fried at the edge of the pond or by a babbling brook.

Once we visited a sawpit and watched this interesting operation. The "Pit" consisted of a depression in the ground in which a log platform was built. The logs were rolled onto this and sawed lengthwise by two men using a "Pit" saw, about seven feet in length. One man stood on the platform, while the other stood on the ground. The sawing motion began and in a few minutes, the log was squared on four sides. Working like this was very strenuous requiring great physical endurance, but people could ill afford equipment used in more modern innovations such as water or oil-powered sawmills. The slabs were cut into firewood lengths, the sawdust used for cattle bedding in winter, and insulating houses. (I had the pleasure of calling in on Eddie some years later in Massachusetts where he was engaged in apple farming.)

Electricity was supplied to the orphanage and hospital by an engine fired by oil and was housed in a building known as the engine house, in charge of which was Herb Simms. He would allow some of us to stand inside the door and watch fascinated as the huge flywheels rotated with a rhythmic thud, thud, thud to charge the generators. It was always cozy and warm, the smell of oil fumes seemed to add to the mystery of how the engine could supply power to buildings several hundred yards away.

Wood-burning stoves supplied heat to the orphanage. The wood was cut during the winter and hauled by dog team from the hills several miles away. This chore was doled out to the older boys, much to the envy of the others. The wood was left on the snow to be stacked teepee style in the spring and dried for fall use. By arranging the logs, we could make a "door" to the roomy compartment in the center and play Indians.

Periodically, a mistress whom we disliked intensely would be appointed in charge. I do remember one in particular. She was very masculine in appearance, even to having a moustache-like growth on her upper lip. In fact, we firmly believed her to be a man masquerading as a woman. Her voice was deep and physical punishment was meted out with a strap to resisting boys. Someone could only have done this with far greater strength than that possessed by the average woman.

As is the custom with boys everywhere, we would make wooden swords and engage in sword fights after the fashion of the Crusaders of Old. We had been studying this period of history at the time. Climbing trees about eight or ten feet high and using lances made of saplings on the ends of which were tied old rags to form padding to prevent injury, we would sway back and forth trying to unseat our adversary following which a sword fight would ensue. At the end of the day, our swords were placed under our beds where they were jealously guarded in readiness for tomorrow's battles.

The mistress at the time, a Miss McCurdy, slept in her room across the hall from our dormitory and must have overheard us discussing the events of the day. Without warning, she entered our room and accused us all of talking too loudly instead of dutifully closing our eyes. Seeing the sword of my brother George lying on the floor, she seized it, and throwing back the bed covers belaboured the boy on his posterior, repeating that we all would be thusly punished. She had picked up the sword by its blade and the blows caused the hilt to separate exposing three sharp, rusty nails holding it to the blade. She continued to rain blows in the region of George's hip until two of the older boys, one of who was my brother Peter, leaped out of bed and restrained her. She proceeded to break the blade in two across her knee and left the room with a remark that she would deal with the rest of us on the morrow. George, in great pain, went to the bathroom where, after sponging the blood off his hip, discovered nail punctures in several places. He subsequently, after undergoing twenty-six operations, had to wear orthopedic shoes on one foot forever.

**Figure 8 Peter Budgell, my brother, before dying of tuberculosis in St. John's Hospital.**

I remember well how Miss McCurdy would send us to the woodpile to saw and split wood by hand in sub-zero winter weather. We wore sealskin boots made of untanned skin, which prevented air from circulating around our feet causing the socks to become cold and damp. The boots would freeze adding to great discomfort. Those of us who were younger would beg to be let into the outer kitchen, but were refused until mealtime. Our hands became numb with cold in spite of "flapping" them against our bodies to restore circulation. It was indeed a happy day for us when Miss McCurdy was duly fired and replaced by others who were tolerant and kind.

Memories of times spent in the orphanage have been, on the whole, mainly pleasant. The incident surrounding my brother George and those of my being locked in a dark cupboard for misbehaving have left me with an inherent claustrophobia and recurrent nightmares. On one occasion, while travelling by train with my wife on a day-nighter, I suddenly awoke yelling, much to the amusement of other passengers. On another occasion, while travelling along the Labrador Coast, in the company of Dr. Grenfell and Dr. Amora, I awoke from my lower bunk and banged my head on the top bunk. Dr. Grenfell hearing this, laughed and said "a guilty conscience, eh Nathan."

In all the Dominions, no subjects more loyal to the Crown could be found than those of Newfoundland. Empire Day called for gala celebrations, one of which gave rise to a very amusing incident involving me personally. It was the custom to give a concert in the school on that day. Ernest Hill, one of the orphanage boys and I were delegated to advertise the event. We carried a sandwich board, a Union Jack and a school bell, which was to be rung loudly and continuously from a point beginning at the harbour mouth to the Church of England, a distance of some two miles. The area in question was across the harbour, so we loaded everything in a small punt and landed proudly on the opposite shore. Appropriate information was outlined in large letters on the board and I, being the younger, was made to carry it. The only drawback was that the board was about as tall as I was a fact that almost proved my undoing.

All went well until we reached a point where a farmer had turned some skittish cows out to forage for early spring grass. The ringing of the bell caused curious residents to stand outdoors and read the message. In addition to the flag waving it proved too much for the inquisitive animals. They staring at the apparition carrying the sandwich board and ran over to investigate more closely. I tried to run in the direction of the nearest house but skidded on a cow flap and this, together with the board's knocking against my knees at every step, propelled me to the ground where I lay utterly petrified while the animals formed a menacing ring close to me. Fortunately, a group of men, in company with Ernest who managed to escape in time, came to my rescue carrying huge sticks driving away the beasts. After a short rest, we continued on our mission vowing never again to play this part with such eagerness. A good turnout at the school helped us to forget the unpleasant experience. However, the recital of Kipling's book, "IF," seemed to have taken on real meaning.

Education, if it could be called such, was dispensed in church-supported schools, and deep religious barriers were erected in the minds of children of various denominations. The emphasis on arts and creeds had a negative effect on the desire to develop an ambitious attitude toward life. Children of the Protestant community of St. Anthony developed a genuine resentment, almost amounting to fear, of the Catholics living in Goose Cove, a nearby settlement. Catholics isolated themselves in small fishing villages along the coast, but came to the Grenfell Mission by boat in summer and dog team in winter to obtain supplies.

On one occasion, when cutting wood on the trail leading from St. Anthony to Goose Cove, we heard the shouts of a driver from the latter village urging his dog team toward us. We were in awe of what might happen should he see us. The snow being at least six feet deep, we immediately jumped up and down close to the tree about to be felled, burying ourselves to our necks and remaining in this unpleasant position till the team was out of sight.

Another time the driver seeing signs of our activity stopped. Crawling out of our hiding place, we engaged in a most warm-hearted conversation. I suppose the skepticism engendered in our young minds was nurtured by joining parades of the "Orangemen" on July 12 to the very limits of Catholic communities extolling memories of the crossing of the Boyne and general misdeeds of our Catholic neighbours ever since. It is refreshing to know that many Protestants, divided within, have joined in establishing amalgamated schools. It is hoped that this spirit will spread to all segments of our society in due course.

Each summer the hospital had its quota of beriberi, TB, scurvy, anemia, and the like, all attributable to poverty- level diets. Many of the fishermen conducted their operations in areas where not enough soil was to be had to make a garden, thus they had to face a long winter on a diet of salt fish, plain white flour, molasses and tea. This was supplemented by hunting game and seals, which, at times, were scarce.

One year, a large French cargo vessel was shipwrecked near Blanc Sablon on the Labrador side of the Straits of Belle Isle. She was carrying five thousand tons of whole wheat, a valuable cargo that was made available to everyone by the underwriters. Since she was high aground it was comparatively easy to unload before the stormy seas succeeded in breaking her up. However, brown flour being only "fit for dogs," as was said in the estimation of the people around, made for few takers. Dr. Grenfell immediately appealed for small hand grinders and obtained a generous quantity from the U.S.A. These he quickly distributed along the coast telling every one of the health benefits to be derived from eating whole wheat bread. The amazing result was that hardly a case of beriberi or scurvy was admitted to hospital the following spring and brown flour became an expected part of the diet. Tuberculosis, however, continued to take its toll due largely to primitive living conditions and contamination. A long but ultimately successful battle was waged against this dreadful disease so that today hardly a case exists.

*Nathan Budgell, DVM*

I fondly remember the Christmas season at the orphanage as we eagerly looked forward to it each year. On Christmas morning, all the children assembled in the biting cold singing carols such as "As with gladness men of old" and ditties heralding the coming of Santa. Another was "pit patter on the roof with quick and patient hoofs - I'm sure it must be Santa Claus, ah yes, Santa Claus he's in his lovely sleigh." At that moment, Santa himself appeared around the point in the harbour in a beautiful sleigh laden with heaps of toys. The fat, rotund Santa, dressed in a red suit trimmed with white fur driving four real reindeer, was a thrill to look at, the bells tinkling on the harness and the muscles of the animals covered with frost. The singing of more carols ensued while goodies were passed around to many happy children.

We found in our stockings Christmas morning, delicious, juicy apples - one only - nuts and candy, rare treats in those days. Having tasted, we, like Adam of old, were determined to have more. The method I discovered at the time was to sharpen a five-inch stick at each end with one end forming a barb. This end was driven into a pole about eight feet long, which in turn was pushed through a transom above the door of the store room in the basement where apples were kept for winter use. Several of the apples were speared and distributed amongst those of us who were conspirators in this foul plan. Kitchen help visiting the storeroom noticed a definite decrease in the level of the barrel and reported this to the mistress in charge who, in turn, directed an investigation. This resulted in our being denied privileges, one of which was the weekly apple on Sunday morning. Needless to say, we were soundly spanked, corporal punishment being carried out by Dr. Curtis. The transom was replaced by a grill, which allowed ventilation, but deterred us from similar pranks.

From Christmas and until January 5, the evening before Epiphany or the Twelfth Night, it was, and still is, a custom to dress in masquerade costumes and go "Gaining." Mummers in England wore similar garbs during the eighteenth century. In this attire, calls would be made on neighbours where simple merriment such as step dancing and jigs were indulged in to the accompaniment of a fiddler and harmonica. Refreshments were served and usually later in the evening, the true identity was revealed. This went on from house to house well into the wee hours. If the neighbour happened to be out, callers would invariably find the table laden with home cooking and liberal liquid refreshments on hand. You just went in and helped yourself. Although this practice is still carried on in some of the outports, it is becoming increasingly less so, partly due to improved transportation enabling people to travel to more distant places to spend the holidays.

The firm of Joe Moores supplied most of the fishing gear to boats operating out of or calling in at St. Anthony. They also owned a large three-masted sailing vessel named the Isobel J. Moore, which loaded salt fish for the Caribbean and Portugal. Wine and rum would be brought back as ballast, the wine being stored in caves under the Cliffs of St. John's, during winter, giving it a flavour envied by connoisseurs. This was probably due to being kept in the hold of fishing ships and then being aged in the cool temperature of the caves for one or two long winters.

The Barbados rum brought back from the Caribbean was the favourite drink of hardy sons of the sea of many generations. Following the cod and sealing fishery meant exposure to the extreme elements of weather and a swig of rum was very welcome on an icy fall or early spring day. The skippers strictly regulated partaking of rum during the fishing season. But when the bankers or schooners were loaded to the gunnels on the return trip from the Labrador Fishery, a keg was usually broken open. The sound of singing and general hilarity broke the stillness in the harbour where the ships were lying to for the night.

On occasion, three or four of us would put off in a punt and row out to the Isobel Moore, or others on the harbour, awaiting their turn to load the fish at the wharf and listen to tales of perilous voyages to faraway lands. We could envision ourselves doing those very things and in our dreams the dangers seemed minuscule compared with the excitement and challenge. Reality was added by gazing skyward at the tall masts and spars on which sails were furled, the smell of tar was everywhere, it being used to preserve ropes, especially those of the ratlines of which ladders to go aloft were made. Ropes were coiled neatly in many places with much of it passing through heavy blocks giving rise to the term "block and tackle."

If the day happened to be a Sunday and at dinner (lunch) time, a kindly Negro cook indulged us with a feed of salt fish or meat, peas puddin' with cabbage, turnip and potatoes, topping it all off with figgy duff and a mug of hot strong tea. The cook on the Isobel Moore was known affectionately as Uncle Syd and seemed not the least bit upset when we came aboard causing a little extra inconvenience at mealtime. By and large, most of the men on the ships were warm-hearted and appeared to enjoy our company. Perhaps it aroused a sentimental longing to see their own children whom they had not seen for many months.

I remember once, on returning from school, we were surprised to see a gang of ten West Indians digging a drainage trench around the Spot Cash Co-Op store. We were told that they had mutinied over squalid quarters on a ship called the Bering Sea lying at anchor in the harbour. A week later, after doing general labour around the village, they set sail laden with fish for Jamaica. They had been incarcerated in the local jail each night under the watchful eye of Uncle Steve Pelley, whom we felt was too kind to be a jailer.

The jail was part of the Post and Telegraph building and was heated by a wood-burning stove. The inmates were made to go into the surrounding woods each day to cut a supply of wood as part of their sentence. Prisoners in for two or three days were fed bread and water only. We deduced that they made up for this during their forays into the woods, stopping in at homes of friends on the way, whose sympathies were almost always with the prisoners. The cell itself was sparsely furnished having only a rough wooden bunk, chair and a chamber pot. An enamel basin stood on a small table in the corner. There were no windows; the only ventilation being through a one-foot square hole cut into the doorway spaced with iron bars. Escape did not seem to enter the minds of offenders, and even when allowed to venture out each day, felt honour bound to return and serve out their sentences.

We would call in to see Uncle Steve on our way home from school and one day he informed us that he had given an inmate permission to go cod fishing in the harbour for a change of diet. A school chum named Harvey Blake asked if we could go along and his answer was in the affirmative. After admonishing the prisoner, to make sure the little boys didn't fall into the water, we set out securing a boat at Joe Moores' wharf and returned in two hours jigging seven nice fish. Some of these were fried on the jail's stove with Uncle Steve taking a couple with him for his family.

After lock up at night, no one was left to attend the jail, figuring that little could happen during the hours of darkness when the inmates were sleeping. This apparent laxity towards social offenders must have borne results because the crime rate, except perhaps in the city of St. John's, was practically nil. One was rarely penalized for drunkenness, the law feeling it was better and less trouble to get the culprit home to sleep it off under a watchful mother's eye than to be admonished when sober.

One dear old couple, Mr. and Mrs. Reuben Simms, I grew to love very much. He resembled physically, Mr. Pickwick from Charles Dickens; rotund, jovial and rosy cheeks like apples. A small stream ran through their property, which was on the road to the Church of England by the land route. The stream had been dammed and several beautiful Mallard ducks with clipped wings were there, their antics, while diving for food, provided a great deal of amusement for us church-going youngsters lingering to watch them.

Whether Uncle Rube thought the orphanage food inadequate, or that as a growing boy I needed extra rations, I do not know to this day. I do know, however, that I seemed to be his favourite, a sentiment shared by his kind wife. They would ask me to hurry out of church and around the harbour to have dinner with them before the rest of the children caught up with me. I broke more long distance records for my age than I can remember.

The table literally groaned under the weight of food of every variety peculiar to the tradition of the average Newfoundlander, to the delight of the eye and stomach of a healthy growing youngster accustomed to the usual orphanage fare. Ducks, alas, taken from their idyllic environment in the stream, and now swimming in rich brown gravy, salt beef, dumplings, vegetables and the inevitable "pease-puddin" with "figgy duff" were served out. Uncle Rube would then sit back in his rocking chair to enjoy a pipe full of tobacco, cutting it from a plug and carefully stuffing it into the bowel.

On these occasions, my only regret was that I hadn't more time because all too soon the voices of the other children, having caught up and passing the house, would reach my ears. When they had safely disappeared around a turn in the road, I would leave my kind hosts and reach the orphanage with the others nonchalantly remarking that I had just loitered on the way. It was not my wish, nor that of my hosts, to reveal the source of my gastronomical satisfaction for fear that the others might attempt to usurp my privileged rendezvous. Naturally, joining the others at the orphanage dinner table, all wondered at my lack of usual appetite.

With the growth of St. Anthony and the resultant increase in crime or misdeeds, the government of St. John's decided to appoint a full-time constable, John Parsons, by name. We would always take a circuitous route around his property which fronted on the Harbour Road for fear that he would discover our excess catch of trout strung on a y-shape Alder twig or "skipper" when returning from Bottom Brook.

He had acquired eight pure white geese and these were accustomed to swimming along the shore intermittently putting their heads under water in search of food. Hoping we could induce them to seek more lucrative grounds in deeper water, we would throw small stones immediately behind them to hurry up the process. Unfortunately, one of the missiles found its mark on the head of the largest goose and it refused to rise. Constable Parsons, missing the bird at dusk, when it would normally come home, investigated in true Sherlock Holmes fashion, discovered the assassins and fined us two dollars each. Since that sum was a veritable fortune, and not having it, we were made to saw and split his firewood for two weeks. Years later when I called on him and brought up the subject, he invited me over to dinner and served what else, but roast goose.

**Figure 9 Sir Wilfred Grenfell and his dog team – 1923.**

Dog teams provided the only means of transportation in winter and during this season were allowed to roam at will in the villages. However, from May until November, during the period when cattle and sheep were around, they were kept in pens fashioned out of stakes driven into the ground to form a kind of stockade. These were built near the stages on which fish splitting operations were carried out. Cod heads and other such offal were thrown into the pens each day, together with a small amount of salted seal meat soaked in fresh water the day before. Of course the pens were never cleaned, but with the first good snowfall, the dogs soon cleaned themselves by rolling in the fresh clean snow. The melting of spring snow soon removed all traces of contamination from the pens. Sheep and cows were allowed to wander at will during the summer and it was not unusual to find three or four animals lying in the middle of the road forcing people to navigate around them with horse and cart.

Cars had not then entered into the picture and I regret to say that since their advent, combined with municipal by-laws, this quaint and unique phase of community interest has almost entirely disappeared. Cars, as I have said, were unknown and I well remember the first Model "T" Ford coming to St. Anthony in 1922, a gift from Henry Ford, founder of the Ford Motor Company.

It was shipped from Boston on the George B. Cluett, a cargo schooner donated to the Grenfell Mission by the head of the firm of Cluett Peabody et al, and in charge, a Captain, Ivar Peterson of Lunenberg, Nova Scotia. He had previously skippered rumrunners in prohibition days and could relate many tales of hair-raising experiences with Revenuers. The "Ford" was duly uncrated under the gaze of curious onlookers and the "Wop," a volunteer worker, having had experience with the contraption, was requested to get it going. He first cautioned us that if we turned on the ignition key, it would blow up, or in terms of the outside world, explode. He only knew the secret, and I must confess this warning sufficed to keep our cotton-pickin' hands off the panel inside the vehicle. It was eventually started with no dire results and everyone watched in amazement as it wound its way to the hospital where Dr. Charles Curtis gave his formal blessing to a new mode of transportation, which would eventually nullify the use of dogs as a means of travel.

In many of the outports dog teams continued to operate until about 1950 and were then replaced gradually by Bombardiers and Skidoos, which although much faster, were subject to mechanical failures. Horses, however, continued to be used for many years after in the narrow "woods" roads hauling pulp and logs to the rivers for the annual spring drive.

I shall never forget the thrill of harnessing the dogs for a day in the woods. They seemed to be as excited as I was. Invariably a race would ensue between the various teams to a point where a path entered the hilly country from the harbour. Shouting phrases such as, "look at the bird or crow," and making trilling noises with the tongue would egg them on to ever-greater speed. Tapping on the bars of the Komatik or sled would also help to increase the tempo and soon every team would strain to reach the single lane leading over Grebes Nest Hill and on to the White Hills. At sundown the teams would return with a full complement of wood to the urging of "home boy, home boy, or, supper, supper, supper," repeated in quick succession in anticipation of a good meal at journey's end. On steep downhill stretches, a "drug" in the form of a chain or a stick inserted between the bars had to be used to slow the progress.

Very few have not heard of Grenfell's adventure on a large ice pan while on an errand of mercy to help a sick child in a small outport called Lock's Cove, about twenty-five miles from St. Anthony. He had to sacrifice three of his favorite dogs. From the bones he fashioned a crude mast on which he flew an old sweatshirt to attract the attention of searchers on shore. The remainders of the team were permanent fixtures on the mission for years after, petted and loved by everyone. The dogs that were killed were named Watch, Moody and Spy. This happened before my life at the orphanage.

## CHAPTER III - SIR WILFRED GRENFELL

From the earliest stage, the orphanage children had to attend one of the churches in the community, namely the Primitive Methodist, or the Church of England. The weather was the determining factor as the former was on the Mission side of the harbour and, therefore, easily accessible even in stormy weather. On the other hand, during sub-zero temperatures and drifting snow in winter, it would be, at times, impossible to trek the one and a half miles over frozen harbour ice, or attempt to row in the Orphanage boat when the harbour was rough. The only other means of getting there was by Harbour Road, a rough and well-worn path having too many subtle attractions. It had deep trout pools in Bottom Brook; luscious berries, when in season; and many other joyous ways for boys and girls to pass the time. We were in the first place, not too eager to arrive at church on time or possibly not until the service was well underway.

As a result of adverse factors, the Methodist Church was graced with our presence. If the reader was made to attend church religiously as a child, he could quite readily sympathize with our having to sit on a hard wooden bench or pew for over two and a half hours listening to the speaker ramble on and on. The low monotone voice often spoke about the terrible punishment waiting at the end of a sinful life. I could never entertain the thought of walking golden streets and listening to unending hallelujahs with never an opportunity to go trout fishing or gather mussels from rocks at low tide.

Heaven, as painted by these dedicated men, seemed very boring and uninteresting. The Church of England, on the other hand, had an order of worship in which the congregation joined to help relieve the monotony. The sermon was usually short, and to the point, enabling us to leave at the end of two hours or less. On occasion, Dr. Grenfell himself would preach the sermon to us, one being about religion having a similarity to electricity with great constructive or destructive powers, depending on how its adherents chose to interpret their faith. His favorite hymn and one that was invariably sung when he conducted a service was "My God, my Father while I stray, far from my home on life's rough way. Oh teach me from my heart to say, Thy will be done." The good doctor was not permitted, at that time, to preach from the pulpit having not been ordained, but rather stood at the bottom near the lectern. I am under the impression that this formality was dispensed with later.

Pews reserved for us were to the left of the aisle and in front. The one immediately behind was occupied by the Hancock family, the dear father and mother later losing three of their children to diphtheria. It seems like yesterday that they stood in their pew, a week later weeping profusely over their loss, while the congregation sang "When morning gilds the skies, My heart awaking cries,

May Jesus Christ be praised." Their faith in the healing power of Jesus was unwavering, particularly in times of deep sorrow.

Dr. Grenfell, when not away on money-raising trips, spent much of his time visiting us in the orphanage. He would take those of us who could endure the walk, on hikes to the fox farm site and Tea House Hill. The fox farm, some two miles away, was established to develop an industry by supplying breeding stock to prospective ranchers in outlying fishing villages. He had, however, no great success in rearing the young pups. With intense competitive fox farming, under more favorable conditions, taking place in Prince Edward Island, he decided against furthering the idea. Perhaps he hoped to re-awaken an interest, on our part, I do not know, but no further attempt was made to revive it.

The "Tea House," of log construction, was erected on Tea House Hill. It was about twelve by eighteen feet, furnished with a small stove, a table and benches. Nearby was a running brook from which Grenfell obtained water for tea. The "Hill" was the highest point in a range behind St. Anthony. From the Tea House could be seen every building on the Mission. At times, while sitting there alone, he must have viewed with great satisfaction the complex forum from which untold benefits were being brought to a needy people.

On our trips he stopped to identify wild flowers which grew in great profusion emphasizing the need for conservation; and read to us from Aesop's Fables, a volume of which seemed to be always at hand. These would be interspersed first with tales of his experiences during World War I and visits to remote communities along the Coast of Labrador.

One plant, which intrigued him, was the Pitcher Plant, now the national flower emblem of Newfoundland and which had a voracious appetite for flies which became entrapped in the sticky substance in the plant's mouth. It grew in boggy areas, and in spite of its gruesome function, was quite beautiful. In addition to the wild, white and blue violets, iris or "Flags," a plant which I have not seen anywhere else, grew. We called it the "scent bottle," growing as a delphinium-like plant but only six inches tall. It gave off a captivating perfume, extremely delicate and sweet. Fleur de Lys (Flags) were found everywhere, and were most likely brought over by French fishermen who fished extensively in that area. Monkshood was found in places where some cultivation was carried on and these too were said to have come from France.

Remains of the French fishermen's summer kitchens, often with artifacts, can still be seen in some areas. A comprehensive book on the flora and fauna of Newfoundland by the Reverend AC Waghorne would be well worth reading. In spring, summer and autumn, every nook and cranny are ablaze with colour of countless hues. The singing of birds and babbling brooks, also apparent everywhere, added to the enchantment of a land revitalized after a long dreary winter.

*Nathan Budgell, DVM*

Sometimes during the hike back to the settlement, bathed in the red glow of the setting sun, the hills casting there long black shadows over the landscape, Dr. Grenfell would tell us of the nomadic aborigines called the "Beothuk" Indians and Dorset Eskimos. These people inhabited the regions of Labrador and Newfoundland, from four to six thousand years ago, the former more recently. He described artifacts found in the area of Port au Choix on the northern tip of the Island. Grenfell was quite convinced that the Vikings had lived here, and it is interesting to note that some forty years later, in 1961, archaeologists unearthed evidence of a Norse village at a spot called L'Anse-aux-Meadows, about fifty miles from St. Anthony.

Prayer was almost always held in the open air, and Newfoundlanders, being a deeply religious folk, were eager to attend. They would be joined by some of the orphanage residents and soon the air would be filled with voices raised in song. The good old Sankey hymns, such as, "Will your anchor hold," "Throw out the life-line," and "Brightly gleams our father's mercy" rang out. The usual ending was with Grenfell's favorite "My God, My Father." His sermons, dealing with the evils of drink and sin, in general were fiery, exhorting everyone to fight the good fight. Many of these simple men had themselves received help for their families from the Mission, on several occasions, and dearly loved this great man.

Many people have asked me how we endured the loneliness of a long cold winter with almost no communication from the outside. When the freeze-up came, about the middle of November, all travel was by dog team. Usually the last mail steamer, her bows reinforced with greenhart and copper would force her way into the harbour after encountering "slob ice" along the coast and thick ice in the harbour itself, about two feet thick. We would watch spellbound as huge, irregular pieces were thrown into the air before the relenting onslaught until a navigable channel was opened for a few brief hours. The last supplies of freight and mail would then be swung over the side, transported by dog team to various centers in the town, the greater portion going, of course, to the Grenfell stores. After unloading, the steamer would then proceed to make a turning basin by going ahead and back, until she had formed a large enough space to turn, heading off to St. John's for the winter. Three sharp toots of the siren were the last steamer sounds we would hear for many months to come.

Roads were non-existent and the sight of my first airplane was almost frightening. It happened during the spring of 1922 when we were in school. Around two o'clock in the afternoon we heard a distant roar and thought the noise to be that of rumblings in the bowels of the earth signifying an earthquake, or some other dire catastrophe at the hand of the Almighty in retribution for the misdeeds of us poor mortals. We, at the behest of our teacher, rushed outdoors to avoid being crushed in case the school collapsed. Lo and behold, what should appear over the surrounding hills, but a bi-plane moving at a tremendous speed. It circled the village a couple of times and landed on the harbour ice. Nothing could contain us, and there ensued a mad rush from every point in the town to observe this bird from the sky.

We, at that time, called an airplane a sky plane. Out of the cockpit stepped Major Fison, President of Fison Fertilizers, and a renowned World War I pilot. He was wintering in St. John's and decided to make a trip with mail to St. Anthony. Our curiosity was such that he graciously consented to talk to us at school the next day answering all our questions and adding a few tales of his exploits during air battles. Since that flight, the airplane has continued to play an important part in every facet of life in the north.

Prior to this, the mail would arrive at intervals by dog team. It was brought to a point called Deer Lake on the west coast, about three hundred miles from St. Anthony. Mailmen using teams of eight dogs delivered it in stages to points along the west coast of the Great Northern Peninsula to St. Anthony. It was supposed to arrive at two-week intervals, but storms and spring thaws invariably intervened. Magazines were often dog-eared; evidence of having been well read during delays, but no one seemed to mind very much.

News of the outside world was received daily by telegraph - the code being ably deciphered by Mr. H. Milley. We would stand in awe as dots and dashes tumbled through the keyboard to be written down and then posted on the wall outside the Post Office wicket. During the Great World War of 1914 this information was eagerly awaited as many of Newfoundland's sons were fighting for the cause of freedom. Ties were very close as most of the population was descended from British stock. Loyalty to the Crown was almost a vice and great sacrifices at the Battles of Beaumont Hamel, Bellieu Wood, and the Marne, will long be remembered in its history. Newfoundland sailors were amongst some of the finest in the Navy.

I clearly remember many of them returning to St. Anthony. The joy was dampened somewhat by sadness of relatives and loved ones whose kin had paid the supreme sacrifice. Awards of valor, including the Victoria Cross, were earned by many of Newfoundland's fighting men.

All of the buildings in the Mission Complex had biblical inscriptions on their facade appropriately emphasizing their specific role. On the orphanage was "Suffer little children to come unto me," on the hospital, "And now, abideth Faith, Hope, and Love, these three, but the greatest of these is Love." On the school was "All thy children shall be taught of the Lord and great shall be the peace of thy children."

A pigeon house was built to house birds for inter- Mission messages and on the Cote was "Oh ye fowls of the air, praise ye the Lord, bless him and magnify him forever." Everywhere one felt the presence of that great Master, physician and teacher who went about doing good and proclaiming "In as much as ye have done it unto one of the least of these my brethren, ye have done it unto Me."

*Nathan Budgell, DVM*

Words cannot suffice to pay homage to Dr. Mason Little, Dr. Joseph Andrews, the eye specialist from California who restored sight to so many blind people on the coast, and Dr. Charles Curtis, the medical superintendent whom I came to know and respect over a period of many years. These "Fishers of men" and true disciples have since gone to their reward where I am sure they were welcomed as good and faithful servants.

## CHAPTER IV - MY BENEFACTRESS - CHRISTINE FELLOWS

Prior to, and during the Great Depression, the back-to- the-land movement was literally interpreted as meaning, at least in Newfoundland, "Face to the sea." Because of the lack of good topsoil and harsh climate, crops for other than personal use were not known. An attempt had been made to cultivate soil in the sheltered regions of Hamilton Inlet at North West River and Mud Lake, but with little success. Hay for winter fodder was grown in the numerous small valleys through which brooks ran. However, with the growing importance of St. Anthony and the prohibitive cost of importing vegetables from Prince Edward Island, it was felt that a worthwhile effort should be made to produce at least part of the requirements locally. The growing of potatoes, cabbage, turnip and the like was encouraged there and in neighbouring communities.

**Figure 10 Hospital Ship "Strathcona."**

Dr. Grenfell was fortunate in securing the services of Miss Christine Fellows of Bradwell, near Great Yarmouth, England, and a graduate of the Swanley

Horticultural College. Her brother, owner and operator of the Great Yarmouth Dry Docks, had outfitted the Mission ship, Strathcona, prior to her sailing.

This ship was donated by Lord Strathcona, President of the Hudson's Bay Company, the Canadian Pacific Railway (C.P.R.), and the Bank of Montreal. He had apprenticed with the Hudson's Bay Company for thirteen years in Labrador and was a great benefactor of the Grenfell Mission. He also donated an additional ship named the "Sir Donald." It will be seen that the Fellows' family had a mutual interest in the Mission.

In 1921, Miss Christine Fellows embarked for Newfoundland on the "Geraldine Mary" owned by the Anglo-Newfoundland Development Company, which operated a large pulp mill in the town of Grand Falls, Newfoundland. She arrived in St. Anthony in the spring and began her work in a spirit of intense optimism.

Her first year was more exploratory in nature trying to decide where best to locate gardens, preferably in areas sheltered from the chilly northeast winds in spring, and having enough soil to sustain growth. Having prepared certain sites, she returned to England and outlined her plans to the executive of the Great Sutton Seed Company, who agreed to supply gratis, as many seeds as would be needed. Their generosity did not stop here, however, and they continued to do so for many years.

Miss Fellows returned again in 1923 and 1924. Having shown an interest in gardening, I was designated to assist her after school, on holidays and weekends. Thus it was that I would spend the whole summer weeding, hoeing and carrying vegetables to the hospital and orphanage. That is when I didn't play truant by hiking off to the nearby brooks to catch trout, a sport which I dearly loved.

I recall that I was the only boy in the orphanage to land a small grilse (salmon) of three and a half pounds at the bottom brook flowing into St. Anthony Harbour. The adulation from the staff and other children when I returned that afternoon was overwhelming. It was quite different when, on another occasion, I landed a huge eel about three feet long. I thought my hook had caught in a rock, but increased strain delivered the hideous creature almost at my feet. Needless to say, I did not bother to disengage the hook from its mouth, but left it wiggling on the rock and invariably made a beeline for home. We were led to believe that an eel would bite and live until sundown even when beheaded. I never bothered to wait and see, although the sun was about to set when I hooked it.

By mutual arrangement, and through the generosity of Berea College in Kentucky, many of the children from St. Anthony's School attended Berea and received technical training. They returned to help in the work of the Mission and in many areas of its activities as electricians, shoe makers and plumbers. Some were also taken to M.I.T.(Massachusetts Institute Of Technology) to be further schooled. I on the other hand, was in for a very different life experience.

The buildings originally erected for Mission purposes were replaced by fire resistant structures over the years. The first was a new orphanage on a wind-swept knoll, east of the old building. I remember on a cold March day, when the earth was glazed with ice during a North-Easter, we would experience great difficulty trying to avoid being literally skidded in an opposite direction, much against our will, on our way to school. The old orphanage was eventually demolished after being used temporarily as an industrial department center where such crafts as rug making, wood working and weaving, were taught. Many of these beautiful products were eventually sold all over the world, providing an income for many families who continued to pursue these vocations in their outport homes after being trained initially at the center.

Figure 11 Hospital patients doing handicraft work with Dr. Grenfell looking on. Peter, my brother is seated right forefront.

**Figure 12 Display of handicraft articles.**

The new hospital of block construction was opened in 1927. It was rated A-1 by the American College of Surgeons, under the able direction of Dr. Charles Curtis, as surgeon-in-charge. He devoted many years of unselfish service to the work on the coast and showed an intense interest in its every phase from farming to education.

Figure 13 The first Grenfell Mission Hospital built in - 1910.

One day in July 1924, while I was helping Miss Fellows with the usual garden chores, she asked me if I would like to go back home with her to England. By this time, my eldest brother, Peter, had returned to Springdale. He secured work with the Anglo-Newfoundland Development Company in its woods operation at Grand Falls. He subsequently acquired tuberculosis and died in 1924.

George, in the meantime, had been in hospital almost constantly having periodic operations on his hip. In the fall of 1923, my sister, Bertha, married and moved to Toronto. She sent for George and there he spent several years undergoing more and more operations and treatments. He studied carpentry and later built cottages and wharves at summer resorts north of Toronto.

My sister, Grace, went to live in Long Beach, U.S.A., with Uncle Joe Langford, mother's brother. He was engaged in real estate, and operated an orange grove in Santa Monica, California. After attending school, Grace entered nursing training in the San Francisco General and Seaside Children's Hospital. She worked in private nursing homes for some years before marrying a Mr. William Adams. After retirement, and three children later, Bill and Grace bought a home near Joshua Tree, (29 Palms). Bill still resides there, as Grace passed away not long ago.

In the meantime, mother had four more children by Mr. John Critch and since she had never visited us at the orphanage, I personally felt rather alienated. So much so, in fact, that when Miss Fellows suggested I go to England, I felt no qualms whatever of conscience at having to leave home. I did, of course, miss

George and Peter terribly, as well as many of the boys remaining in the orphanage with whom I had an almost brotherly relationship.

Time seemed to fly from the day Miss Fellows informed me of my impending trip. I visited many of the people I knew in the town who would almost always add, "Well, Natan bi, you're goin' a long piece from 'ome".

The great day finally arrived, September 12, 1924. We embarked on the coastal steamer Earl of Devon, or known to us as the "Early Devil". It made the run from St. John's to St. Anthony, thence to Battle Harbour on the Labrador Coast and on to Humbermouth, now a part of the City of Cornerbrook. This is and was the site of a large pulp and paper mill and was a center for a now defunct Newfoundland Railway.

At Humbermouth we waited overnight for the train which would arrive about noon on the following day, the day I would have cause to remember all the days of my life. I had never seen a train but a vivid impression had been created in my mind after seeing a print of Turner's famous painting from the Tate Gallery in London.

## CHAPTER V - ENGLAND

At last I was to see, and actually ride, a real Puffing Billy, which had been instrumental in spreading civilization to every part of the world. When the actual moment arrived, I was terrified, awed and yet thrilled and excited. Standing on the station platform, I could hear the train, its whistle alerting everyone that the Great Newfoundland Express would soon pull in with a hissing of steam and screaming of brakes. As she came around the bends and coves and into the straight of way, the magnetism of the sight almost impelled me to jump out onto the tracks.

Engines at that time were run by steam, coal-fired, a sharp contrast to the streamlined diesel locomotives of today. Soon we were boarded to the shout of "all aboard" and seemed to fly literally through the countryside. Around sharp curves and hills, over bogs and along sandy stretches near the ocean to the familiar clickity, clack of the wheels over sections of track in the direction of Port aux Basques. Here we were to catch the boat to Canada. I must confess it was not a smooth ride, but I enjoyed every moment. The fact I say "on to Canada" is because, at that time, Canada had not yet joined Newfoundland, this happened in 1949, making them very separate.

About twelve hours later, we arrived at Port aux Basques' Newfoundland Ferry Terminal, which connected by ship with North Sydney, Canada. Newfoundland, being a self-governing Dominion, the usual customs inspection was carried out and we boarded the passenger steamer S-S Burgeo for the twelve hour trip across the Cabot Strait, a distance of about one hundred miles. We encountered quite rough seas and the small steamer would disappear into the deep trough of the sea never, as I feared, to rise again. After a hair-raising experience, and much seasickness, we sighted Cape North and the mainland of Canada to the relief of everyone on board, although the Captain remarked "that was nuttin' bi."

At North Sydney, we entrained for Quebec City, an enchanting trip through a wonderland of vivid autumn colour. Crossing the famous bridge over the St. Lawrence River modeled after the firth of Forth Bridge in Scotland, we entered the old walled City of Quebec. We spent a week there visiting the Old Fort, Plains of Abraham and Wolf's Cove, site of the battle that was to end French domination of Canada. Having made all necessary arrangements for my legal entry into England, we embarked on the Empress of Britain, which was a staggering sight to a small boy from a Newfoundland outport, and arrived in Liverpool on September 28, 1924.

Entraining for Southport, we stayed with Dr. Malcolm Fellows, brother of Miss Fellows, and a practicing physician. While there, we visited the town of Chester where I saw the Sands of Dee, where Dr. Grenfell spent much of his boyhood. One week later, we journeyed to Great Yarmouth, a large fishing center on the east coast, and on to Bradwell, about three miles from where Miss Fellows lived.

I have never, by any stretch of the imagination, believed that such a green and pleasant land existed. Coming from the rock bound isle of Newfoundland where farming as such existed, with a constant struggle against long winters, foggy springs and short, wet summers, it was beyond wonderment to be in a land of verdant green pastures. To see untold numbers of sheep and cattle grazing in every field forming a patchwork mosaic of every shade of green and brown with neat hedges bordering the pattern was amazing. Lazy streams meandered through the countryside and farmers with their plough teams were turning over the soil in preparation for seeding the following spring. Although late in the year, the song of birds seemed to fill the air. Newfoundland had its rugged beauty too, comparable to Scotland. It commanded an inherent love on the part of its sons and daughters having their roots interwoven with those of ancestors from the British Isles.

Bradwell a small hamlet of some two hundred souls had a schoolhouse built of flintstone. It had a Church of England some four hundred years old with Rev. W. Walker in charge. He appeared, without fail, at nine o'clock every morning opening school with a hymn and scripture reading. Miss Fellows could be referred to as one of the upper middle classes having a dwelling called Cygnet Cottage.

Some cottage! I was overwhelmed by the look of this house. It was like a mansion to me, like the Waldorf Astoria is to grown-ups. It was surrounded by four acres of land divided into a shrubbery, kitchen garden, fruit and flower garden and two small fields, one of which contained a hen house for about twenty hens, with the other for recreation. I spent many happy hours in the latter with some friends playing soccer on weekends.

**Figure 14 Dudley Howard and myself.**

One of these was Dudley Howard whose father operated a market garden growing luscious strawberries. We spent many enjoyable hours under the pretext of scaring the birds away. His father must have deduced that more than birds were decimating his crop and finally told us to stay away. He substituted a long length of stout string leading to a number of tin cans on a post in the middle of the patch. His buxom wife would vigorously tug at it at intervals during the day. Whether it was effective or not I cannot say, but Mr. Howard was strongly suspicious that night crawlers - and I don't mean worms - were responsible. It is said, stolen fruit tastes sweeter. I do know that I have never since tasted strawberries more delicious.

Many of the apple trees were trained on wires strung horizontally on posts, as was a large fig tree on the south wall of the carriage shed. Two gardeners, full time, were employed and another came during the fall and spring. A red brick wall divided the fruit and flower area from the shrubbery. Against this background was planted pink and white phlox, delphiniums, and other flower varieties. Usually petunia and heliotrope were in the foreground. Along one of the walks was a border of lavender, and any area which Miss Fellows considered unsightly, was covered with yellow canary creeper or clematis.

At the wall end of the garden was a well-kept lawn, one side of which bordered the small field and had a covered stoop with its front end open to the sunshine. At one end of the stoop was a small carpenter shop and fruit shed; the latter was windowless, but ventilated overhead. It was here that we placed our winter supply of apples from the garden on sweet smelling straw, being careful to have them arranged so that they were not touching. I remembered being very fond of two kinds - the Golden Russett and Pippin. Pears were also stored here, but plums and berries were made into jams and preserves. One must really experience personally the scent filling the evening air from the many flowers in the flower section. Lavender, heliotrope and nicotine combined, to permeate even into the living and bedrooms.

The shrubbery area contained many beautiful flowering shrubs, as well as holly, yew, and laurel. In one corner was a sunken garden, surrounded by ferns and as the front door opened into this area, a large rose bed was developed here. In spring, tulips would first bloom under the rose bushes followed shortly after by large beautiful red roses. On either side of the front door were two borders in which wallflowers would bloom in profusion in late summer.

In the kitchen garden were grown all vegetables from artichokes to leeks, required for the house. It also contained a potting shed where young plants in spring were potted in flats and pots, later transferred to our greenhouse, which was built in a lean-to fashion on the whole south wall of the house. While I learned a great deal about more refined gardening in England, I was required to do very little in that area because of the excellent help employed.

Cygnet Cottage itself was built of brick and contained five bedrooms each having a fireplace. It had a main room with a huge fireplace an adjoining dining room, kitchen, scullery, and maid's quarters. The coach-house and stable were joined to the goat house where four Toggenburg goats were kept. The stable and goat house bordered on a large concrete yard in one corner, which housed our hand pump. The whole property bordered Church Street separating it by a red brick wall approximately two hundred feet long and five feet high. The remainder of the property was separated from neighbours by a large private hedge. It was especially high and thick where our fruit garden abutted the next property where there was the local pub named the "Rising Sun."

I could not conceive why living within three miles of a large city, we had no running water, or electricity. Water was pumped by hand to a cistern in the attic and fed by gravity to the kitchen and bathroom. To take a bath, we had to half-fill the large iron tub, light a flat kerosene-type stove with jets and then push the stove under the tub which was standing about ten inches off the floor. When the water was warm enough, one had to take a hurried bath before it cooled off. Miss Fellows said more than ten minutes in warm water was bad for one's health.

Before enrolling in school I had the greatest pleasure of touring the famous clipper ship Cutty Sark. Miss Fellows on boarding the ship had a certain unexplained glint in her eye. I managed, in a short time, to see first-hand most of the nooks and crannies of this great vessel. Ten miles of rope was used for the sails and a figurehead called Nannie stood out on the bow with a sea radiance. After touring the Cutty Sark, Miss Fellows had train passage booked to Norfolk, to my amazement, to the home of Captain Richard Woodget, the most well known and longest serving Master of the ship. He had a snowy beard, weathered face, and talked at length with Miss Fellows over tea, about other times and places they had spent and seen together. He knew well of Newfoundland, Dr. Grenfell and the harshness of the Atlantic Ocean. On leaving Captain Woodget, I noticed a quietness come over Miss Fellows, and, I think I now know of the glint that I detected on the deck of the Cutty Sark.

On leaving England after my education Miss Fellows gave me two carved pieces, one in teak the other in mahogany. She explained they had been gifts to her from Captain Woodget years before. They had been "chipped-carved" during the approximate two hundred days it took to voyage from Australia to England.

I spent three days visiting Miss Fellows' brother in Southtown, a suburb of Great Yarmouth. His name was Henry and he operated the Great Yarmouth Dry-Docks and Shipbuilding Company. Many of the fishing "drifters," and coastal freighter boats were built and launched from here. I spent many happy hours attending launchings and watching boats being built.

On Monday, October 6, 1924, I attended the Bradwell Village School, under the supervision of an able but stern schoolmaster by the name of Mr. Ernest Jacques. On the first day, seeing that I was having difficulty learning my pounds, shillings, and pence tables, and obviously trying to demonstrate his wide knowledge of world currency, said in front of the class "Nathan has known only cents and francs," whereupon I interjected "No Sir, cents and dollars." "But you did not live in the United States" he had answered.

Newfoundland was closely allied commercially with Britain and France through their large fishing fleets, which went to Newfoundland every summer, and readily accepted currencies from these countries. Jacques could not comprehend how the U.S. dollar could possibly play a hand in Newfoundland commerce.

Day after day, I struggled to master twelve pence, one shilling - twenty pence one and eight pence and so on through tables, which ran on interminably. When it came to stones, quarters, rods and the like I felt the end had come and wished I had never said yes to Miss Fellows. I was put in a section of the one room schoolhouse and given periodic tests until I began to acquire a working knowledge of this archaic system. In fact, Mr. Jacques, feeling that I needed more isolation away from the snickering which I could plainly hear on the other side of the curtain, due to my Newfoundland accent, let me occupy the small living room in his house. It was joined to, and part of the school complex. Because of my neufy accent I was always asked to recite "Drake was in 'is 'ammock and a tousand miles away, 'art dou sleepin' dere below?"

Slung 'atween the round shot and listenin' for de drum and dreamin' all de time of plymet 'O."

I never regretted being able to acquire a basic knowledge of English education at Bradwell School. The embarrassment resulting from taunts and jibes directed at me would have been much worse, I fear, in a larger institution. I gathered that the traditional concept of English fair play was to be found in those who had reached the age of discretion. Children are the same all the world over tending to enjoy hurting one at a disadvantage.

School being opened by the Reverend W. Walker was closed by Mr. Jacques with the singing of either "Now the day is over" or "Abide with me," to the accompaniment of a pedal organ which, after giving us the key, was abandoned at about the middle of the first verse. The Lord's Prayer was then recited and school dismissed with the admonition "please no trouble until your return on the morrow."

The evening shadows had descended at this hour, and on my way home, a gang of boys would follow on my heels remarking "hey, you double Dutchman" and other names. This often would result in a rousing scrap. However, two of the boys, feeling sympathetic, came to my rescue and woe betide the ones who tried to molest me in the future. One of them, a Dudley Howard and I became fast friends. Mr. Jacques, on hearing of the attitude, tried, after meting out appropriate punishment to the offenders, to explain to them that my dialect was akin to that of the old Sea Dogs during the Elizabethan era, still spoken in remote corners of Devon, Cornwall and Newfoundland.

Arriving home, my despondency was not lessened in an atmosphere created by the glow of kerosene lamps, the globes of which had been dutifully cleaned of smoke by the maid before reuse every morning. One was kept on a wall bracket in the hall downstairs, assigned to me on retiring. It had a small globe that was less likely to blow out from the downdraft created by each step while ascending the stairs. The lamp was left on a small table and turned quite low all night on retiring, in case of an emergency. The cold, damp winter weather helped little to cheer one up, and seemed to penetrate into every corner of the house. The last half-hour of school was devoted to the singing of songs, and the words of one imprinted themselves indelibly in my memory. They told of a little kettle swinging on a hanging chimney hook singing merrily in the dreary wintertime, which to say the least was true.

Each night I would recite poetry, read, do homework or be quizzed on work to date. Sometimes a game of chess or checkers would break the monotony while sitting in front of a cheerful coke fire in the drawing room, the heavy drapes drawn tightly over the doors and windows to keep out the night draughts. Miss Fellows suffered from chilblains, a common ailment peculiar it seemed to the English, although I fortunately never experienced that discomfort.

We acquired a wireless, primitive by today's standards, but the latest thing then. Manipulation of large coils brought in the BBC. Master's Voice type speakers amplified the sound and we put an extension into the kitchen where every evening about twenty villagers would arrange themselves on chairs to listen to the "BBC News, Direct from London" at seven o'clock. We had the only radio in the village at that time.

The school taught gardening as one of its subjects. We were required to tend a plot, twice weekly, during school hours, and as often as we wished afterwards. If we saw an unusual bird or even a common thrush, a drawing had to be submitted with a summary of its activities while on the garden plot. Not being very artistic, I am afraid some of mine looked more like prehistoric monsters.

Learning our Catechism at school, church attendance was a must. The routine of donning my best shorts, Eton jacket and collar, round straw hat with a black band, suede gloves and silver topped cane, was strictly adhered to. The hat was secured to my lapel by a black braided cord in the event that a strong gust of wind would remove it, and had to be doffed whenever meeting my elders, especially the ladies. Miss Fellows, suitably attired, proudly accompanied me to our reserved pew. I still treasure a small leather bound book of Common Prayer, which she gave me on my first Sunday in Bradwell. It beseeches the Almighty to bless our gracious Queen Mary, Alexandra the Queen Mother, Edward Prince of Wales, and all the Royal Family. Later in the prayer for the King's Majesty to behold our most gracious Sovereign Lord, King George. After an hour or so in which Reverend Walker expostulated at length on Greek mythology, and anthology, having little relationship to the saving of sinners, the service ended with a recessional played on the organ by Tubby Martin.

He was our neighbour, owned and operated a genuine steamroller fired by coal, used to patch up country roads and also to run the threshing machines during harvest. Being the church organist Tubby paid me a shiny silver sixpence to pump the organ during his weekly practice. I would stand transfixed when he started up the engine, releasing a lever to spin the huge flywheel from which a wide belt connected to the rear wheels, set the machine in motion. The stack, located over the boiler section, reminded me of the early locomotives belching out their long smoke trails over the lonely prairies.

The usual procedure after church but before lunch was to feed the hens and collect warm new laid eggs from the nest boxes. The thrill of this event remains with me to this day. Although we have since owned and operated flocks producing over sixteen hundred dozen eggs daily, the excitement of finding perhaps eight or ten eggs in our old-fashioned nest boxes, being pecked by a cantankerous hen who resented me feeling under her for yet another egg, was a unique experience.

Miss Fellows always arranged to have a cold roast on Sunday to lessen the Sabbath duties. A rolled rib roast of beef was the order of the day, except at Easter, when lamb with mint sauce was eaten. After lunch two or three school chums and I would walk to Gorleston-on-Sea to enjoy a stroll along the promenade, breathing the fresh sea air blowing off the North Sea. The beach at Gorleston was safe for swimming, but at Great Yarmouth, about two miles away, were treacherous rip tides and undertows.

The latter beach, however, contained what was said to be the remains of Peggoty's Hut, made famous in Charles Dickens' "David Copperfield." It consisted of a schooner sawn in half, turned upside down near sand dunes at the harbour's mouth. It was well tarred, having a door with two windows cut into the side. The interior, although the worse for wear and tear, showed definite signs of its having been used as a habitation. It was first brought to my attention by a school chum, while we were strolling he merely remarked, "that's Peggoty's Hut where Peggoty lived."

Few people gave it more than a passing glance, and it was only three years later while working at Somerleyton Hall in Copperfield county, that I took a keener interest in that interesting book. We then visited Blunderstone and the rectory with its rookery, and traveled along the same road, which David did to catch the coach to London, stopping along the way at the small Post Office to leave a message for Peggoty from Barkis saying, "Barkis is willing."

Bradwell Church, some three hundred years old, issued a monthly magazine for the parish. Miss Fellows took it upon herself to deliver it to the more remote parishioners; most of whom lived in an area called "the Doles." I would accompany her on Saturday afternoons along a route, which took us through winding country lanes bordered by thick green hedges. These were full of birds' nests in springtime with blackberries and raspberries in late summer. We traveled over fields, which almost always had a style providing access to a neighbouring field or footpath. We entered farmyards where hens, ducks and geese led a life unthreatened by automobiles, and would spend awhile with the kindly farm wife chatting over a cup of tea; then on past small water holes where timid moorhens lived contentedly with their broods of offspring. Some of those we visited were either too old, or physically handicapped to attend, and a full report would be made as to their welfare on our return.

It was on one of these jaunts that I became interested in egg collecting, taking along a shoebox with compartments of varying sizes to collect eggs en route. I took one from a batch of five and found the parents were not alarmed to the point of desertion, a fact that I was careful to check in subsequent visits.

One interesting old lady by the name of Miss Drown lived in a small one-room cabin near a railway underpass. She was not a member of the church and lived the life of a recluse with over twenty cats. The cabin was tar papered and not more than ten feet by fifteen. She would pass our house every day on her way into town to obtain scraps from the butcher, which went on for a number of years until the authorities decided to intervene, the cats were taken away and the old lady put into a home with more suitable quarters.

In the fall of 1926, Miss Fellows decided that I had obtained suitable grounding to attend an institution of higher learning. In September, I was enrolled in the Edward Worlledge Central School located at Southtown, Great Yarmouth. The town of Great Yarmouth derived its name from the River Yare. It had its source at Downham Market, which flowed through Norwich, and on to the sea. The shipyard was about one mile from its mouth, and was responsible for the building and repairing of fishing boats or "Drifters," repairing lightships for Trinity House in London, and responsible for their operation. The school was near the residence of Mr. Henry Fellows at 76 Southdown Road. It was very convenient for me, as, I could spend an hour there, meandering around the dockyard at lunchtime.

Some of us, at times, were given an assignment to visit ships from many countries moored at the quay, asking about their cargo and destination which brought memories of "The Ships of Yule." Russian ships would bring lumber and return home with herring in barrels. Norwegian ships brought lumber and returned with manufactured goods, Spanish ships brought fresh fruit returning with fish. In contrast with the rules and procedures of today, the trading atmosphere was friendly amongst all sides. Immense quantities of herring were caught on the Dogger Banks in the North Sea, then shipped salted in barrels to Russia.

During the herring season, usually in the fall, many drifters from Aberdeen would come to Yarmouth to work the fishery, bringing their complement of "Scotch fishing girls" to clean the herring. It was said, much to the chagrin of the local lassies, that they could split and clean three to one of the locals. I became convinced of this when watching them work. They would stand in front of a long splitting table with bins full of fresh herring, twelve hours at a time. It was remarkable how quickly the fish disappeared into the barrels nearby. Many of the boats would enter the harbour unloading their catch at pier side. They would swing their catch in large tubs onto the wharf by means of a boom. If the catch were not designed for splitting, it would be barreled and salted for the foreign market.

During this operation, some of the herring would spill onto the wharf. If we happened to be there at an opportune time, on our way home from school, we would dart under the tubs of herring and quickly retrieve a dozen or so to take home. The owners seemed not to be concerned so much about our filching as about our getting hurt by a tub full of fish crashing down on us.

Mrs. Henry Fellows, or Maggie, as she was called, evidenced a motherly interest in me. She had a son, Manning, who was more interested in theatricals than shipbuilding, much to the disappointment of his father Henry. He became quite proficient in acting, appearing in Shakespearean productions at the Maddermarket Theatre in Norwich. Mrs. H. Fellows was active in politics, and was an Alderman in the town council. Every year she organized a clothing drive for needy families of the county.

Schoolwork became more involved, with much more homework. Miss Fellows thought I should buy a bicycle to lessen the time traveled on foot to and from school. On foot there was too much to distract me on the way, and at least lost time would be made up. The problem, however, was financing. I had a small money box at home on which was written at Miss Fellows' insistence, two sayings, namely, "Have more than thou showest; say less than thou knowest" and "Neither a borrower nor a lender be." Well in the face of this what could I do to attain this objective?

Miss Fellows firmly believed that nothing was fully appreciated unless it was hard earned, and I knew full well that I had to start from scratch. She, however, pressed half a crown in my hand admonishing me to make it grow to forty-nine pounds eight shillings. She no doubt contacted her brother in Southtown, because on the following day, he asked me to weed his garden on Saturdays for three shillings a week. On top of this, an older gentleman friend of hers, having a sore knee, advised that the doctor said it should be massaged with an embrocation every night. So, after school each day I proceeded to do just that for half an hour. In retrospect, and in the light of subsequent knowledge in this regard, I wonder if that were his whole aim. It seemed to arouse a physical response of which I was totally innocent at that time.

Before long, green pound notes in exchange for silver began to appear in my moneybox. Since I had accumulated over thirty-three pounds twelve shillings, Miss Fellows felt that with the approaching deadline for school imminent, added the remainder. One afternoon we went into Gorleston proudly purchasing a new Raleigh three-speed bicycle. It had an oxy-acetylene lamp, and was as bright and shiny as a new pin. The only condition attached to the extra help in acquiring it was that I keep it sparkling. Every Saturday I would spend at least two hours rubbing and polishing every exposed part. Getting to school was no problem, and, the following summer, I used it to go back and forth to work at Somerleyton, seven miles from home.

**Figure 15 My new Raleigh three-speed bicycle.**

*A Newfoundland Son*

Somerleyton Hall, home of Lord and Lady Somerleyton, consisted of a large estate of some four thousand acres, comprising of extensive parklands in which were kept deer, pheasants, and a home farm with its herd of purebred Jerseys. The garden, made up of vegetables, fruit and flower sections, was well tended by a large staff under the supervision of Earl Hanson, the head gardener, under whose tutelage, I learned all the rudiments of basic gardening. I started off the day by cleaning his shoes, then weeding the walks on my hands and knees, a most painful chore. However, after a month, I was given the work of gathering vegetables for daily use at the Hall. These were in turn taken to the house on a two-wheeled wheelbarrow where I would invariably be treated to cakes and lemonade. One day I was given the task of pruning plum trees trained on wires on a south wall. Hearing voices, I turned to see the Somerleytons with Lady Anne Cavendish and the head gardener approaching. Seeing me they halted and I could plainly hear His Lordship remark "that boy is one of our colonials from Newfoundland," here to learn horticulture.

As it happened, I could not have spent a more profitable summer anywhere. Three of us lived in a "Bothy" or small dwelling, one of whom was the assistant head gardener. My last duty daily was to crush coke in a hand crusher, providing heat to the greenhouses on chilly nights, by means of ducts. My only objection came from the dust arising as a result. It contained dried urine and was used by the workers in emergency situations in a secluded area at the back of the garden. Exotic plants of every kind were grown on the grounds and in the tropical garden. Many of the flowers were meticulously cared for, in preparation for the annual show at Chelsea.

Under the supervision of the game warden, one or two deer were selected for killing each year. A platform would be constructed in a tree, the deer driven past at great speed. The marksman rarely failed to miss from his perch. Pheasant shoots were also held, with persons of high rank being invited. Our job during these shoots was to "beat the bushes" while advancing in a row. This caused the birds to fly up and over the woods to waiting guns on the other side. Next day we were asked to comb the underbrush for any game which may have been wounded or lost. For each bird found, the warden would give us a brace (two) of rabbits.

Many Saturdays were spent at the ancient sport of coursing. Owners of whippets, a small greyhound like dog, would meet at a place called Fritton, near Somerleyton, and retire to a large lowland area called a fen, adjoining pasture lands on higher ground. Owners would station themselves in pairs with their dogs at the far end of the field. Meantime, others would go into the fen knowing it was a hideout for hares (leveritts) and rabbits during the day, shouting and beating the bushes. The game would immediately run into the fields where the whippets would be let loose. I have never seen more elusive animals almost turning on themselves to avoid being caught. In the two years I was there, I don't recollect one being cornered. It did provide lots of fun and we did not consider it cruel.

*Nathan Budgell, DVM*

It was arranged that I do something every summer to increase my knowledge of animal husbandry and general farming. One was spent on the farm of David Harham at Craethorne North Yorkshire, about eight miles from Stockton on Tees. This was a mixed farm; its mainstay being a flock of some four thousand black-faced Scotch Sheep, a very rugged breed, seeking out an existence on miles of rugged moorland near the farm. A shepherd's hut was located about the center of this area. The sheep were watched over by two border collies and one English sheepdog, who would bring them into an enclosure every night. I spent several nights with the shepherd listening to stories of his experiences, searching all night for lambs born in hedgerows during an unexpected blizzard in late March or early April. The flock was brought into the lowland area in early December. After being sheared and dipped in spring, were turned out onto the moors for the remainder of the year.

I found work on the farm very strenuous, having to arise at five in the morning to work all day and into the night during harvest time. I milked ten cows of a herd of twenty at that hour and again at four in the afternoon. I would harness up Topsy the pony, and run the milk into the railway station some seven miles away, where it was taken to Northallerton for processing and bottling. I received as compensation for my work half a crown, (about fifteen cents) weekly, plus board and lodging.

I was rather pleased when Miss Fellows arranged, that I return home, preparatory to attending Chadacre Agricultural Institute at Harest, near Bury St. Edmands, in Suffolk, England. Miss Fellows had arranged that I relax a few days before enrolling at Chadacre. One diversion was to go out shrimping with a man from Southtown. The procedure was to lower a drag or kind of scoop to the sandy bottom about a hundred yards off the beach, drifting out towards the Scroby Sands some three miles off shore. Periodically the drag would be hauled aboard with its harvest of shrimp.

Everything went fine for awhile. It was a pleasant day with a slight wind from the southwest and we seemed to be "in the shrimp." About two hours after leaving, the wind increased and veered around to the Northwest, with waves rising about three feet high. An especially strong gust broke the small mast to which the mainsail was fastened, and the whole piece of wreckage fell halfway into the sea, still held to the boat by one or two ropes. All we had was the spinnaker, a small sail at the rear of the boat. The skipper's helper managed to pull the mainsail and mast into the boat. The shrimp drag was left out to help steady the tossing boat now being blown rapidly onto the treacherous Scroby Sands. After almost capsizing twice, we grounded on a sand spit, where two other boats, having seen our predicament, came to our rescue. One had an auxiliary engine and towed us into port. We managed to save the catch, but what to me was a most frightening experience, was to the shrimp boat skipper, all in a day's work. He admitted that he had meant to brace the mast as he thought it might "break off sometime." Needless to say, he gave me an ample supply of the delectable crustaceans to take home.

On two other occasions I enjoyed full uneventful days of exhilarating sea air and sunshine, listening to stories of shipwrecks and shown mast tops of former wrecks slowly being engulfed by the sea, mute testimony to once proud defiant coastal vessels. Around us at all times the sea was abustle with other shrimp boats and herring drifters gleaning a rich harvest from the sea, supplying the enormous domestic and foreign market. A famous processed herring is called a Yarmouth Bloater, a smoked product having a quality that only those knowing the secret can impart. Who would have thought that forty years later the real wealth of the North Sea would be determined by the discovery of immense basins of "Black Gold" which today supply largely the needs of the British Isles. It certainly is a far cry from the Great Yarmouth Coal and Coke Co. Ltd., which supplied fuel for fireplaces, found in almost every household and gas for street and household illumination.

One of my fondest recollections is that of having watched the old lamplighter, on a bicycle, stopping to light the street lamps at dusk every evening. In winter, I was usually on my way home from school at that time, and he always greeted me with a cheery "Good Night."

Some of my happiest memories, however, are those of summers spent on the farm of Morton and Lucy Woolston at Burgh Castle, some nine miles from my home in Bradwell. Morton had spent four years, during World War I, in the Royal Horse Artillery, a fact of which he was very proud. He kept two of the finest Percherons around the countryside, which he used for general farm work. Tractors were few in the thirties, with most of the farm work done by horses. In fact, all of the produce was taken to market on a horse-drawn dray or cart, and other goods such as beer and lumber were delivered by teams of two to four horses. Most of the streets were paved with cobblestones and this, together with iron shoes and iron-shod wheels, made a lot of noise. Before the days of my bicycle, we would occasionally jump on the drays for a free ride home from school. It was while attempting to get on one that a chum of mine slipped between the wheels crushing the flesh to the bone just above the knees. He was taken to the hospital where surgeons dexterously repaired the injury and after four months hardly a scar remained.

The coming of the first mower into the area created quite a sensation. It was horse-drawn and was purchased by a farmer called Saxe Bond. Behind his back we called him Sexy Bond, being handsome and having a great way with the women. He was the owner of the fastest pony in the area, every weekday taking five cans of milk into the town dairy. Since he traveled along the same road and time as I did on the way to school, he would attempt to keep pace with my bicycle doing twenty miles an hour, often succeeding.

Before Saxe acquired the mower, all hay was cut with a scythe. Four of us would go into the hay or oat field on a warm August day, and cut a swathe with the swing of the scythe, proceeding about ten yards. The next in line behind did likewise, until four of us were advancing along the side of the field rhythmically swinging our implements. When the cut crop had lain to dry for a few hours, men, women and children would "Bind" the crop by shuffling their feet under the stalks until a sizeable sheaf had been formed. It was then bound, using a tie made of several stalks, following which it was stooked, or stood in rows of eight bundles each four to a side to dry. After a week, when dried, they were loaded on a farm wagon and taken to a point near the barn for threshing. My job and the dirtiest one at that was cleaning the dust laden chaff which penetrated into my eyes and every crevice of my body. Awns from barley were the worst, itching and driving me to the point of exasperation. During 1928, the first binder was purchased. It was horse-drawn, of course, and the crop was cut and tied into sheaves in one operation.

Rabbits were very plentiful; usually having their burrows underground in hedgerows bordering the field. They would invade the grain field to feed on succulent clover and fallow grain toward harvest time. Of course, when the binder would start its operation, they would keep moving toward the center of the field until the area became so small that they would have to bolt for their burrows. Waiting there of course, were many people and dogs, their excitement increasing as they espied rabbits leaving the ever diminishing refuge and dart back again when sighting the army of humans and canine. The inevitable moment came when they simply had to make a break, the scene being one of pandemonium. A lot of rabbits escaped, but many found their way into a pie the following day. A Sunday menu ritual on the Woolston farm was delicious rabbit pie made only as Lucy Woolston could make it. Often, at night, we would do a little poaching by netting the entrance to the burrows, and sending ferrets down an unnetted hole to flush the rabbits out. Sometimes the prize would amount to over twenty rabbits. All of these apparently cruel sports were beneficial in curbing the rabbit population, which fed on young growing crops. It was interesting to find that later on the government found the problem so serious that they introduced a deadly viral disease called Myxomatosis, to curb the population.

The Woolston farm, located at Burgh Castle, was named after an old Roman fort on the banks of the River Yare. One of his fields was enclosed on three sides by the walls of the fort, about twenty feet high with round bastions or towers at each corner and in the middle. The walls, four feet thick, were made of flintstone and cement, and commanded a section of the River Yare seven miles inland from Great Yarmouth. The walls were covered with a profuse growth of ivy. Ploughing during the spring and summer months often unearthed Roman coins, pottery and arrowheads. I saved them for a number of years, but eventually they were lost in my travels.

During the Easter holidays of 1928, Miss Fellows and I toured the south coast of England from Dover to Biddeford in Devon. It was said that unless a Newfoundlander visited Poole in Dorset, he had not been in England. From Portsmouth we boarded the Victory to see the spot where Nelson had died. It was of particular interest, because Nelson had attended the school at North Walshan near Great Yarmouth, which we visited often to see the school desk on which he had carved his initials.

Lyndhurst in the New Forest was very picturesque and the wild ponies were everywhere. A monument to Rufus the Red felled by an arrow while hunting had been erected not far from Lyndhurst. At Swannage Bay, a granite memorial told of the victory of Alfred the Great over the Danes. He was the one who supposedly burnt the cakes. Salisbury Cathedral and Wimbourne Minster with its library of very old books interested me, and Stonehenge perplexed me. The vision of those Druid priests sacrificing humans on an altar sent cold chills down my spine.

In 1929, Miss Fellows took me to Europe during the summer break from school. In Zermatt, Switzerland we stayed at the Zermatten Hoff Hotel. I arranged to join a group of tourists who had hired a guide to aid them on their climb of the Matterhorn. Passing the Lady of the Snows Church on the lake, we finally reached a hostel that was located at four thousand feet. This was as far as the group had planned to go, so the guide and I continued on to the top. Following the arduous climb to the summit we viewed a spectacular splendour of clear skies with snow-covered peaks all around. I surmised there was room for about fifteen people at the peak. I spent twenty minutes absorbing the feeling of accomplishment and awe before starting our descent. This was an experience I have never forgotten!

I also did some cliff climbing on the Gornergrat, and enjoyed many hikes through the beautiful Alps. In almost every upland pasture, Swiss women could be seen contentedly knitting and tending their Brown Swiss cows. One especially quaint practice was to drive goats through the streets milking them at the door. I wonder if this practice is still carried out in this day and age, when it might well be considered unsanitary.

In Venice, Italy my main interest was St. Mark's Church, although I did enjoy scenic trips in the Gondolas. The city itself held great meaning as I was studying Shakespeare's "Merchant of Venice" at the time. The rest of the summer was spent at the cottage in Sutton. I lazily fished for Bream and Perch while watching the Wherries on their way to Norwich with raw mustard later to be processed into famous Colemans Mustard. Visiting Goodwin's store to be given a handful of sweets by two of the dearest people I have ever known made each day complete.

*Nathan Budgell, DVM*

The fall of 1929 found me, once again, at Chadacre for my final year. I enjoyed getting back to the soccer eleven, participating in cross-country running over fields ploughed and unploughed, through thorny hedges, rivers and woods for a distance of ten to twelve miles. I was very proficient in sports and held the long distance record for the school, and the Health and Strength Club in Great Yarmouth. Jogging was an everyday routine and one, which I maintained even after returning to Labrador. It was an accepted way of keeping fit and not a newly discovered fad as one is led to believe nowadays.

In April 1930, I graduated from the Chadacre Agricultural Institute, seventh in a class of forty-four. We had been thoroughly taught tin-smithing, horse shoeing, animal husbandry and other pertinent subjects in preparation for any chore arising from routine farm work. In his closing remarks, the Chairman, Earl of Iveagh, referred to my attainment saying that he was especially pleased to note that a lad from Newfoundland who, until he arrived in England, had never seen grain growing or been associated with farming in its real sense, had through persistent application attained a high standing at the Institute. He wished me God's speed in returning to a harsh environment where all the skills acquired at Chadacre would be put to the test.

# CHAPTER VI - BACK HOME

Following graduation, I visited the Head Office of the Grenfell Association in London where I had the pleasure of meeting Sir Wilfred. He received a Knighthood from His Majesty the King, and was afterward referred to by this title. I also met Mr. Job of Job Brothers & Company who donated the first cottage hospital to the Mission of Indian Harbour on the Labrador Coast and also Miss Katie Spalding to whom I had been endeared since a child. At this meeting my immediate future was discussed. It was decided that I would return to North West River, 120 miles inland from the Coast of Labrador, the site of a hospital, school and small boarding home for students in winter. Here agricultural possibilities were, if at all, better than on the soil of the bare, cold coast, constantly washed by the frigid Labrador Current. My stipend was set at five hundred dollars a year with board and lodging. Late April, and most of May, was spent preparing for this great event.

Only one who has lived in England can imagine my feelings of having to leave that green and pleasant land in the spring. Songbirds literally filled the air with their music; bluebells, primroses, and daffodils covered the earth with a mosaic of colour and the heavy perfume of lilac was everywhere. No more could I look forward to idyllic weekends at the cottage in Sutton, gliding in our boat past creaking windmills, and watching the antics of numerous waterfowl while fishing for fat bream.

After purchasing guns, knives, heavy work clothes, boots and a portable manual record player with an ample supply of records, classical and semi-classical, books by a good selection of authors, all packed in stout trunks, it was with a feeling of nostalgia, and almost resentment that I embarked from London on a ship called the "Geraldine Mary". She was owned by the Anglo-Newfoundland Development Company carrying pulp and paper to England, taking machinery and building materials back to the Botwood Port of Grand Falls where the mill was located. Perhaps not until that moment did I realize how much I was going to miss my benefactress and how inadequate were my parting words of thanks to one of the kindest and most understanding persons I had ever known. We wept profusely, of course, but they were tears of happiness and acted, as a catalyst to an endearing friendship kept alive by correspondence until the good Lord took her to her final rest as a result of cancer in 1934.

I arrived off the fog-bound isle of Newfoundland on June 5, 1930, passing perilously close to enormous icebergs and floe ice. The fog was so dense, and since it was before the days of radar, the Geraldine "hove to" off Fogo Island sounding her siren at intervals to warn other ships of her presence. Toward dawn, we saw the light on Fogo although we could hear the fog horn all night. The morning came on grey and chilly, but everyone on board was relieved, knowing that we could at least see the icebergs, instead of having to detect their nearness by the echo from our siren. We immediately started up the "Run," as the inlet leading to Botwood from the ocean was called, passed islands with quaint names such as "Right in the Run" or, "Pick Me Up Harry" until twenty miles lapsed and we sighted Botwood.

On board were Mrs. Hugh Cole and daughter returning from school in England. Hugh Cole, superintendent of the mill, was a bundle of energy. He assigned a man to help carry my luggage to his waiting private car and off we went to Badger where I stayed for two days at his comfortable home, thence to Springdale to see my mother. The forty miles over land to my hometown was something for the record.

The "Bus" was a decrepit taxi, and the "road", an improved footpath hardly wide enough for the car, was full of boulders with streams crossed by a crude bridge made of logs. The service, if it could be called such, was operated by a Mr. Enders of Springdale who felt that he could not endure the mental and physical strain of such a trip without the support of good black rum which he would sample at intervals. At the end of the road a boat, also operated by Mr. Enders, conveyed us to Springdale, a distance of seven miles. We braved a gale, which caused six-foot waves, but did not daunt the determination of our valiant skipper, the rum bottle being well drained before we embarked. We narrowly avoided some small islands at the entrance to Springdale, but being assured that there was plenty of deep water, we docked at the wharf. I brought half of my luggage on a rack attached to the car roof and was told that the remainder would arrive on the next trip in two days. It did, on June 12, after spending three days with my mother.

A note to mention as a point of interest to the reader, mother spoke of seeing a huge snake-like creature she and others watched often in the bay. It turned out to be what they called in Newfy dialect a "Canger Heel" or in plain English a Conger Eel. Its serpent-like head would lift above the water and was reported to be some sixty plus feet in length. This maintains the truth of sightings by mariners and of their serpent tales.

Saying our good-byes, I caught the coastal steamer "Prospero" on which, after steaming through heavy masses of ice, I arrived at St. Anthony. Many stops were made on the way to unload supplies for the many fishing villages found in almost every cove. In many cases there were no wharves and the ship had to anchor off shore while small boats came out to be filled with goods swung over the side by the boom.

At the wharf I was met by Sir Wilfred Grenfell; Dr. Charles Curtis; and Dr. Moret, who was in charge of the hospital at St. Mary's River on the Labrador Coast. After being duly billeted in Newell's Hotel operated by Johnny and Olive Newell whom I had known since childhood, I spent several days waiting for the opportunity to sail on the Mission Ship "Maravel" for North West River. I helped Sir Wilfred clean his fresh drinking water dam of the silt accumulation.

We would dig the silt and wheelbarrow it to a point on the gravel path around the house. Between these chores I horse-harrowed several small fields near the barn, helped Dr. Curtis milk cows, build pigpens and repair fences. The pigs of the Tamworth breed, had been given to the Mission by Lloyd George, a former Prime Minister of England, who owned a large farm in Wales. They, in addition to supplying food, helped clear land in confined areas.

On June 29, I was again helping Sir Wilfred at his dam when suddenly the fog, which had been too thick for navigation, began to lift. Grenfell, throwing down his shovel remarked "come on Nathan, let's go." Within an hour we set sail in the good ship Maravel for Battle Harbour some seventy miles across the Straits of Belle Isle on the Labrador side. We encountered much floe ice and several icebergs, many of which had grounded in the shallow water. The small harbour of Battle Harbour was, in fact, "choked to the hilt" so we decided to heave to for the night, tossing gently on the water. Sir Wilfred sat on the edge of his bunk thinking I supposed of future tasks still left undone until I fell into a deep sleep.

Battle Harbour itself, was under the direction of Dr. and Mrs. Moret, and one of the first posts established on the coast to aid fishermen bound for the more northerly fishing grounds. It was built almost entirely on the rocks and was home to those very rugged people, and to persons dedicated to subjugating everything else to a life of tolerant isolation. The trading store, Baine Johnson & Company, was the center of activity supplying all the fishing vessels and bringing a large three-mast schooner into the Port in autumn to buy and load salt fish for export to foreign markets.

Early the next morning, we headed for St. Mary's River, eight miles north, where, in a secluded wooded inlet, the Mission had decided to erect a hospital and other needed services to replace the one at Battle Harbour. The advantages were fresh running water, lots of wood, and freedom from the fog, which almost always enveloped the Coast.

On July 1, we headed for Cartwright, site of a cottage hospital, school and Hudson's Bay Company Post. The flag of the Hudson's Bay Company and the Union Jack floated proudly in the breeze as we entered the harbour. On the 140-mile trip from Battle Harbour, we sighted icebergs of every size and description imaginable, with colours and hews of pale green, dark green, blues and white. They appeared like huge cathedrals with spires reaching over two hundred feet into the heavens. Others had huge arches caused by erosion, while still others were solid masses of rectangular ice weighing many thousands of tons on which were nestled clusters of sea birds. Sir Wilfred, on one occasion, and in the company of two experienced deck hands, launched a dory and proceeded to explore the arches and alcoves of one gigantic berg. Those of us on deck watched in horror for fear that the mass would roll over sending them to a certain doom.

Sir Wilfred left us at Cartwright, so we headed north the next morning for Indian Harbour at the entrance to Hamilton Inlet, a 120-mile arm of the sea. It drained torrents of water from the mighty Hamilton, or as the locals called it the "Grand River," flowing from the Hamilton Falls, or more recently named "Churchill Falls. Other rivers such as the Northwest, Kenemish and Goose contributed to the volume, draining the untold number of lakes in the great interior. Indian Harbour, so called because of the rock profile resembling an Indian in repose at the north end of the island, was chosen because of its fine anchorage, a halfway point between Battle Harbour and the cottage hospital, with a small general store.

While in harbour, skipper Will Simms told me of a rather practical joke he and his crew played on one of the residents a few years before. As he said, they were "dying" for a meal of fresh (meaning meat) and their craving was soon to be fulfilled. One night as he and two others were walking up to the hospital, they saw in the beam of their flashlights numerous pairs of eyes shining like diamonds in the darkness. A kindly-intentioned lady from the United States was convinced that goats were the answer to the extreme poverty in that part of the world where almost no fodder existed, and donated a number of the animals to the Station at Cartwright. Up fishing with her family for the summer at Indian Harbour, she thought that a few goats would provide fresh milk and in the fall could be transported to Cartwright, or taken back home to Conception Bay in Newfoundland for breeding purposes. Of course skipper Will Simms knew nothing of this and concluded they were semi-wild until one, unfortunately, came right up to him. The temptation was too great; he and his crewmates seized the poor animal, which in no time was stewing in a large pot in the galley. All other evidence of the dire act was sunk overboard in a weighted sack. Next morning, a troubled lady appeared at the wharf looking for the animal. She solicited the help of the crew of the Strathcona who conducted a wide search of the island to no avail. They convinced the lady that the goat must have fallen over a steep cliff to certain doom. The incident seemed to weigh on skipper Will's conscience for many years. After telling me of it, he said "Well bi, they were sent to provide milk and meat, so what's the odds".

At Indian Harbour, we were informed that we would have to take the body of a man who had died of tuberculosis to North West River for burial. Further investigation revealed that death had occurred about a week before our arrival. He had been put in a rude coffin made of fir that was not particularly water or air tight. To preserve the body rock salt used in curing fish had been liberally packed around him. When we arrived the salt had started to leech from the seams emitting a very unpleasant odour. The anticipation of a trip up the inlet of ten to twelve hours under bright sunshine filled our minds with grave misgivings, and we wondered of the amount of fresh air we would enjoy on our trip inland. It would all depend on which way the wind was blowing. We decided to put the coffin on top of the wheelhouse, which was the highest point and where the breeze would do its utmost. Tying handkerchiefs around our mouths and inserting long poles under the coffin, we walked, or rather staggered over the rough ground to the Maravel. Using the deck, winch and sling, we deposited the burden on the roof of the wheelhouse. It was secured by planks and ropes prior to our setting off for North West River. We called in at Rigolet, site of a Hudson Bay Company Post in charge of which was George Budgell, an uncle of mine.

Rigolet looked very picturesque with its red and white buildings, well kept and managed. Realizing that the only way to tolerate the very unpleasant odor surrounding the boat was speed, we headed through the narrows and into the broad inlet. Our rate of about twelve knots left the stench far behind and we were fortunate in meeting a west wind which accelerated the back drift. Hamilton Inlet lies in a large basin surrounded by the Mealy Mountains on the south and a Height of Land on the north and west. On the western range located today are Labrador City, Wabush and the Churchill Falls Power Development.

As we approached the Mission Station, I was struck by the almost sub-tropical vegetation compared with that found in the frigid atmosphere of Indian Harbour. It was lush and dense, some trees being over sixty feet tall, overlooking golden, sandy beaches. The area was dominated by a lone ominous peak called by the Indians "Mokamee" or God of the Heavens. It was between two to three thousand feet high and usually surrounded in a ring of mist, adding to its mystery.

The salt by this time had melted and was leaking quite profusely from the coffin. Seeing the relatives waiting on the wharf, we decided to let them unload the unpleasant cargo. They took it to the cemetery where a short ceremony by Rev. Lester Burry, United Church Minister, returned the mortal remains to the ground, with the singing of "Safe in the Arms of Jesus." I hope the Great Physician did not have the same aversion to a partly decomposed body being ceremoniously placed into His arms.

I later learned that the poor man had left four small children behind, eventually all succumbing to a dreaded disease which exacted its toll on many areas of the coast. Coming from St. Anthony where modern methods had been instituted to help combat this dread disease, I could not help feeling that the motivating personality behind this Christian effort would have been greatly saddened by such pathos. No one but a truly devoted worker would have realized that this was only a part of the routine. The Son of God continually exhorted His followers to "Do the works of His Father" adding "By their works shall ye know him." St. Paul said, "I have fought the good fight". He did not say, "I have directed the good fight." Grenfell's true work was in his doing, not especially in what he said, believed, or thought he believed. It is in this context that his, and that of his co-workers, must be viewed.

*A Newfoundland Son*

# CHAPTER VII - NORTH WEST RIVER

At North West River I met Dr. Harry Paddon, his charming wife and later Jack Watt, a native Newfoundlander who had been in charge of maintenance around the Mission for some years. The village itself was spread along a sandy spit of land bordering a short swift river, the Northwest, emptying the waters of Grand Lake into Lake Melville. On the west bank lived a few trappers, but in summer a Band of Montagnais Indians also camped there. A small Roman Catholic Church had been built without pews or seats, the worshippers sat cross-legged on the floor during the service. A priest visited them from St. John's during the spring bringing a boatload of useless knick-knacks much sought after by the Indians, receiving in exchange, many valuable furs. In fact it was said that the choice ones were kept for him, much to the chagrin of the Hudson's Bay Manager. A well-used phrase was that the letters H.B.C. stood for "Here before Christ," so perhaps the withholding of quality furs was retribution for past misdeeds.

The Indian Chief's name was Pastene, the father of two very beautiful daughters with long flowing black hair. I first met them when they were about eighteen, but three years later I noticed a definite aging probably due to the exposure to the weather and strenuous trekking through the country in winter. Their father had a rare characteristic of azure blue eyes.

On the Mission side of the river was a Hudson's Bay Post, supplying the trappers and buying their furs. There was a hospital, school and small barn where necessities were stored. A hundred yards or so from the barn was a teachers' cottage where I lived. It consisted of four bedrooms, large living room and kitchen that served also as a dining room. The furnace, wood-burning, consumed large birch logs at a phenomenal rate in winter. About two hundred trappers with their families lived in houses strung out along the length of the sandy, spit of land, most of them having a little wharf where they tied their canoes in summer. These wharves were painted white in spring resembling floating ice packs which served as camouflage while hunting geese sat on them in great numbers on the waters of the inlet. In fall the colour would change to green to blend with the landscape.

The Indians were, in large part, called "Company Indians," many of them proudly wearing a metal or button to denote this. The Company supplied them with everything from tents to food and money was rarely paid for furs. All credit was well repaid in kind, the interest being calculated against the value of the skins. In early days, the value of a rifle was determined by stacking as many furs as possible, well pressed, against the height of the weapon. One thing, however, which can be said is that the Hudson's Bay Company looked after the natives. Basically all they needed was food, clothing and shelter. They were not able to spend money, except at the Hudson's Bay Store, and money being the root of all evil, it was perhaps just as well that they had no root.

After surveying the farm potential and inventory, I wondered just why I had been delegated to start work here. The community was far removed from sources of fertilizer and supplies, the former greatly needed for the very sandy loam. The cost of bringing artificial fertilizer was prohibitive; nullifying the objective of trying to produce cheaper produce than that imported. Near the coastal areas sheltered coves and inlets, people gathered quantities of seaweed or kelp that they mixed with caplin or fish offal providing a valuable substitute for farmyard manure. At North West River we had neither. The caplin, a small smelt-like fish swarmed ashore in thousands while spawning in June on the coast. They did not come in as far inland and seaweed could not be economically brought so far inland. Dr. Paddon, however, was full of optimism and said that ultimately the cows could provide enough manure, an opinion with which I could not readily agree. He spoke of supplying other Mission stations, such as Indian Harbour and Spotted Islands, but I could not envisage the success of such an effort having regard for the facilities at hand.

I suggested that since the Indians had little to do, we could employ them to clear some land about a quarter mile behind the village, which in turn could be moderately productive. They would be aided by an old horse called Maggie, who had never been harnessed; a carryover from a defunct mill operation across the Bay at Kenemish. It seemed that two horses, one a stallion, were abandoned at the site, so Jack Watts went over to round up the critters. The stallion was wild and mean and after chasing him into the water, he had to be shot. Maggie submitted to being lassoed and was towed behind the motor boat to North West River, a distance of ten miles.

Since I had helped break a few heavy hunters in England for Sir Thomas Buxton, Minister of Agriculture, I decided Maggie could be a useful co-worker in clearing the land. I made a collar with traces that I attached to two logs and tried to lead Maggie by a long rope. She strenuously objected but after infinite patience, I managed to convince her that she would be rewarded with a handful of oats every time she did the right thing. After a month or so, I felt she could be harnessed to a small plough which I found amongst a few other farm implements at Mud Lake, some twenty miles up the inlet from North West River at the entrance to the mighty Hamilton River, the site of another defunct lumber mill.

At both Mud Lake and Kenemish, the operations had been quite expensive, but transportation difficulties, together with the isolation, eventually contributed to the abandonment of both sites. Mud Lake, especially, showed a genuine attempt at farming. Quite a large tract of land had been cleared and when I visited there in July, the temperature in the well-sheltered fifty-acre field was 102 degrees Fahrenheit. All around the site, trees stood seventy-feet tall, with the grass chin high. Wild raspberries and blueberries were growing in profusion and

I wondered why the Mission had not decided to locate the farm there. The soil was of a deep loam in nature ideal for crops. Of course the growing season was short, but at least a month earlier than on the coast. In my second year, I discussed the possibility of seriously reviving the farm at Mud Lake through the United Church's sponsorship. I saw Reverend Lester Burry, a well-known minister covering the Labrador Coast in his launch called "The Glad Tidings," from the North West River Headquarters. He too sensed the possibilities and tried to interest his superiors in St. John's to take an active part in the venture but they, thinking nothing could be grown agriculturally in the "land God gave to Cain," failed to become enthused. I retrieved the plough, a spiked harrow, and one or two collars with harnesses from the old farm site.

I actually fell in love with Mud Lake. The mouth of the river teemed with trout, and more magnificent scenery could not be found anywhere. In spring and fall, thousands of geese and ducks made a stopover here. To me it seemed a veritable Eden in an immense wilderness. I can well realize how early settlers opening up the Great West must have felt on reaching similar areas after crossing miles of desert.

Kenemish at the mouth of the Kenemish River, some fifteen miles from Mud Lake, was not as richly endowed. Trees, which were its prime concern, grew in abundance but the land was rather stony and hard to cultivate. Apparently in its case, the failure of the supply ship to arrive with food stores, due to an early freeze up on the coast, caused a lap of exodus on the site, leaving a large clothing store well stocked for one hundred men. In charge of the site was Angus McLean, a tall, likeable Scotsman. He lived a lonely bachelor life at Kenemish but was provided with ample necessities by the Company. Angus would fraternize with the Indians on their annual sojourn at North West River and Chief Pastene claimed a relationship with Angus, a fact attested to by his blue eyes.

My first year at North West River was spent clearing land aided by any Indians who cared to help. They would show up at about ten o'clock in the morning and quit about noon when the sun became unbearably hot. Every tree stump had to be manually removed after chopping the root mooring and, at times, it took the strength of eight or ten men to haul them out. After this, picks and shovels were used to remove roots trailing under ground. When I considered the ground sufficiently ready for ploughing, I harnessed Maggie to the small plow. She did fairly well for several bouts on roughly one acre of prepared land, and then decided she had had enough. She felt the environs of the barn about half a mile away a much nicer spot. Without warning, she galloped away over the fields, the plough bouncing on contact with every obstacle. I was powerless following her as fast as I could, but by the time we both arrived at the barnyard, the handles of the plough had been broken. I set to work shaping and splicing new ones, starting the whole procedure again.

By the end of September, four acres had been cleared, the Indians by this time, tired of the need for constant application entirely foreign to their nomadic way of life, left in early October having garnered supplies necessary for a winter of trapping from the Hudson's Bay Company. They melted away into the vast wilderness abounding with fur bearing animals and game.

Three cows had been brought from St. Anthony to start a herd. One, a fourteen-year-old short-horn called Molly, still milking, one Swiss brown named Melba, having calved in May and yielded almost seven gallons of milk daily, and the third a Holstein heifer calf. I urgently requested a bull to be shipped before freeze up in early October, and one arrived by coastal steamer at Rigolet to be ferried the last 120 miles on the small Mission launch, thirty feet in length.

Jack Watt who was an experienced seaman undertook to supervise the operation but found he had a problem when he discovered that the crate containing the bull would not fit into the boat and the animal, therefore, had to be tied in a space between the engine and the rudder. All went well for about fifty miles when a severe squall struck sending huge waves over the boat forcing Jack to seek shelter on the opposite side of the bay in the lee of the land. The bull became panicky and began to thrash around pulling the ring out of its nose. To make matters worse, the boat pitched violently in the shallow water near the shore and hit bottom, losing its rudder in so doing. As a result, it had to be steered by dragging the grapline or rudder alternatively over each side of the bow. All was confusion so Jack decided he had no other recourse but to dispatch the poor animal, which by this time was quite unmanageable. One could imagine the consternation when we accepted the news, as it would be utterly impossible to obtain another before the following summer. Fortunately the cold October weather preserved the meat affording a plentiful supply of fresh beef well into the spring. The tragedy though acute was not without its benefits.

In spite of obstacles encountered in land clearing over four acres were made ready for sowing in the spring. My plan was to cut the oats green or just before ripening so that the grain could be retained and fed to the stock in late fall. This worked very well providing valuable additional fodder. A sizeable vegetable plot was cleared on arrival at the station and supplied a good quantity of turnip, cabbage and potatoes for winter use. We brought a liberal supply of Paris Green and bi-chloride of mercury to combat pests, which seemed to invade the garden immediately on transplanting the young plants. To offset the possibility of a major disaster in the garden, we hoped to enlarge and improve upon in the following year, I decided to order, through Jack Watt, a quantity of insecticides to be sent in before the last boat in October.

In August I had taken five men to Mud Lake with scythes and cut seven tons of hay in a fifty-acre field. After curing we stored it in one of the tumble down farms until we could fashion a crude raft of logs to transport it to the Mission settlement. The craft measured forty by thirty feet, three layers deep, lashed together with rope. The hay was loaded and towed ten miles to its destination. In addition we cut more hay along the shore near the settlement, providing an ample supply for the winter. I had heard of people having one or two cows running short of hay at the end of winter before the grass began to grow, resort to the feeding of willow and alder twigs and could not envision such a dire need on my part.

The cows continued to milk until April of 1931, then gradually dried up. Five young pigs had been sent from St. Anthony in the fall and quarters were made for them at one end of the barn. The floor was made of planks three inches thick. One night in early January we awoke to the shrill squealing of pigs, dressed hurriedly and raced for the barn. We could hardly believe our eyes at the sight of four huge husky dogs wriggling out from the area in which the pigs were kept. On entering, we found that they had gnawed a hole five inches in diameter through the floor and succeeded in seizing one of the unfortunate animals by the hind leg. It was so badly mauled I had to kill it. In the morning we procured some roofing tin and covered the pen area on top. There we laid two-by-six-inch planking. Since we had no electricity, I kept a storm lantern lighted every night at the end of the barn and this seemed to discourage the dogs.

It was not uncommon for temperatures to fall to fifty degrees Fahrenheit below zero in mid-January. Eskimo dogs or huskies were the sole means of transportation in winter. Frequently a mournful cacophony of howling broke the silence of a moonlight night. One lonely dog would begin at the far end of the village only to be joined by others until a loud eerie chorus would ensue lasting for perhaps five minutes. They rarely howled on a dark night, probably given rise to the saying "dogs howling at the moon."

Dr. Paddon made frequent trips to outports, some one hundred miles away by dog team in winter. A Delco Electric System provided electricity to the hospital, but all other buildings used kerosene lamps.

The school principal, Miss Marjorie Baird graduated from Oberlin College; Miss Betty Lorimer, a grade teacher from Chicopee, Massachusetts, together with Dora Soward, who was with me at the orphanage several years earlier, also lived in the cottage. Marjorie was a typical school-marm, quite sedate and fully in charge of her position, but Betty was to say the least a complete extrovert. She would love to don snowshoes and tramp through drifts visiting neighbours, listening to their experiences and joking about how awful it was to manipulate the "things" in heavy snow. Occasionally in fall, I would take her to snare rabbits, a sport she seemed to enjoy. Years later, I met her brother who was Attorney General of New Hampshire. I regretted having to terminate our relationship the following autumn when I left the mission temporarily to go trapping. I guess you might say she was my first love.

During the spring, prior to leaving for the "trap grounds," we started several hundred cabbage plants in a miniature green house, fashioned from home-made materials. There was anticipation of surpassing the bumper crop of cabbages the previous year. My order of insecticide had not arrived in the fall and I dreaded to think what damage could occur to a growing crop without its aid. This meant that I had literally no effective means of combating what I felt was impending doom. The plants had to be in the ground in early June and navigation in these frigid zones did not enable supplies to be brought in until late June or early July. By this time, grubs would have done their worst. I explained this fact to Dr. Paddon and asked for an explanation as to why the order had not arrived, although sent for in plenty of time. He seemed at a loss and so nothing else could be done but await the inevitable. The only other possible approach was to use soot and salt between the rows to inhibit the movement of the grubs. Salt might, however, damage the roots but anything was worth a try.

On June 2, we transplanted two hundred plants and ten days later, seeing no sign of damage, decided to plant three hundred more. One week later, with still no evidence of damage, we applied soot between all the rows. On June 22, while making my early daily inspection, I discovered twenty-three of my precious plants cut off neatly at ground level. Disaster had struck with a vengeance. I quickly employed as many boys as possible and had them inspect every square inch of soil for grubs, which if found were gleefully dispatched. The enemy however, outwitted us, and at the end of the three weeks, not more than fifty plants survived. It was too late to start anew and when discussing with Dr. Paddon his ire could not be satiated. Maybe he thought that after my intensive training I could work miracles. I was informed that my services would no longer be required. Why he became so incensed over this single matter I do not know to this day.

The beets, onions, Swiss chard, lettuce, turnips and potatoes were all coming along fine, although the turnip did give us a little trouble. The outfield seemed due for a bumper crop and the hay field at Mud Lake was doing well. I wrote Sir Wilfred Grenfell telling him the whole story and in late September received a sympathetic letter and a note adding, "Christ has work for you to do in St. Anthony." Perhaps he knew the temperament of Dr. Paddon whom I found to be quite subject to childish tantrums.

Sir Wilfred's letter arrived about freeze-up time in the days before air transportation or roads. I wrote him saying that I could not get out until spring but would as early as possible. Paddon realizing my predicament said I could stay around until the following May or June working for board only, I declined and started looking for something to occupy me for the winter. Maybe one of the reasons for Dr. Paddon's attitude was the fact that the "great depression" was beginning to affect adversely the financial position of the Mission. He thought the previous staff could well carry on the work without having to pay an additional five hundred dollars a year for my services.

## CHAPTER VIII - TRAPPING IN LABRADOR

While visiting a well-known trapper named Syd Blake, who was preparing to go into the woods on his trap line, I was asked if I would like to go along on a share-basis. His fur path was some 150 miles long beginning twenty-five miles north from North West River at Cape Caribou on Grand Lake stretching both east and west of the Lake for roughly seventy-five miles. It ran over muskeg in the mountains, across brooks and rivers and through dense forests harbouring every type of fur-bearing animal from the humble muskrat to martin, lynx, wolverine, otter, fox, mink and bear. Game animals and birds such as caribou, rabbit and partridge were in abundance. "Tilts," or cabins, located about every twenty-five miles serviced the fur path and it was expected that an average man could cover this distance while tending traps on snowshoes each day.

The suggestion sounded first rate to me and we shook hands on the deal there and then. On September 5, we went to the Hudson's Bay Company Store to see the Manager called the "Factor" a native Newfoundlander named Bernard Aisle. He was enthused with the idea and outfitted us with everything necessary for a successful winter trapping. A new thirty-thirty rifle, carbine type, twelve-gauge shot gun, traps, heavy clothing and food, food and more food were supplied. It was all transported in several canoe loads and taken to a winter house at the narrows located at Little Rapids, three miles up the Lake from the village.

It was here that Syd moved his family, his wife, mother and sister-in-law for the winter. The two young boys stayed with relatives in North West River where they went to school. The only heating was a big rectangular stove in the middle of the kitchen. This was filled just before bedtime, but usually died out before morning causing the house to become so cold that frost formed on the walls.

All of our supplies had to be taken from this point by canoe to the main tilt at Cape Caribou twenty miles away. It meant crossing the four-mile-wide Grand Lake diagonally on each trip, a tiring task during a head wind. Supplies were left here at the eighteen-by-twenty-foot until they could be delivered to the smaller tilts after freeze up.

Between the trips up the Lake and before the freeze up, Syd decided we would make a brew of spruce beer which he contemplated selling to Indians who invariably called at his house on their way to pick up supplies at the Post. Having no other place to put the keg containing spruce needles, Bakeapples and yeast, he suggested a corner of my bedroom leading off the kitchen as an ideal and accessible place. Days went by and I could plainly hear the "mixture working." A wooden bone had been driven into the hole at the end and the keg was laid horizontally on two-by-fours with blocks to keep it from moving. At around three o'clock one morning, when all was still, a loud c-r-r-r-rack, like the firing of a powerful gun echoed through the building. Thinking we had been invaded by

Indians having gained knowledge of the brew we, or rather, I, jumped out of bed and went slithering across the floor in a sea of beer foam. Syd arrived at my door seconds later and I thought he would die laughing. Nothing daunting, he rolled up his pajama legs and waded barefoot into the mess with a shovel, putting it all back into the keg, once more placing it in the same corner. He drained off some of the fluid and we sipped a good portion while cleaning up the slimy mess which had penetrated every crevice of the wooden floor. At that stage, the brew tasted fine, two weeks later we sold it to callers for ten cents a glass which they drank while sitting on a bench in the kitchen.

Food supplies for the camp consisted mostly of flour in fifty-pound bags, tea, sugar, baking powder (from which with flour and water we made sourdough bread) fat back, salt and lard. It had all been safely stored in the main tilt before freeze-up. After, it was taken in easy stages to each small tilt when we went along the fur path.

By the time the snow started to fall, we had caught a goodly number of muskrat, beaver, mink and fox. The former was trapped by setting the trap under water and the latter by setting traps along a fox path easily discernible in the moss and grass where they searched for food. Sometimes, we would put out a set of traps, using a large one at the center, on a mound, where there was evidence of mice burrowing a nest for winter, and where foxes dug to locate the tasty morsels. Around the perimeter toward the center of this mound, we would place a set of smaller traps. When the fox or foxes proceeded to investigate the tasty piece of salt herring or beaver pride, (a soft, reddish-brown powdery secretion of penetrating odour obtained from the perpetual follicles of beaver, dried and rubbed on the trap) they would invariably be caught in one or two of the smaller traps. The musky odour of "beaver pride" seemed to have a strange fascination for the foxes and, at times, a pack of four or five would fall victim to its scent and be caught. Once, in fact, we did actually catch four in one set when supplying the tilts along the fur path from the main depot.

We usually carried 150 pounds of flour with the aid of a head strap, a leather belt two inches wide passing around the forehead supporting one fifty-pound bag between the shoulders. Another bag would be deposited across this one on the shoulders and the nape of the neck. This left the hands free to carry smaller items including a small axe and rifle. Portaging in this way was very difficult and tiring and was employed between the ponds on the trail.

Whenever a fox or lynx was trapped, a quick blow between the eyes with an axe handle stunned it. In this state of unconsciousness, pressure was put on the chest by kneeling on it so that the animal could not breathe soon expiring. Shooting, of course, would have ruined the fur.

The usual routine before snowfall was to arise at five o'clock, drink a mug of tea and eat sourdough bread. The bread was often fried with either bacon or rabbit stew left over from rabbits we had snared and cooked the day before. Any leftovers were put in a pot and hung from nails driven in the rafters, naturally refrigerated in the freezing temperatures. It was an unwritten law that a supply of wood for at least four or five nights, sufficient flour, tea and matches be left at all tilts in case of emergency. Woe betides any person, Indian or white, who violated this law.

Cooking was done in a small rectangular metal stove. Candles were used for lighting and the floor and bunk were covered with ends of fir branches inserted one under the other, upside down, to form a springy and sweet-smelling mattress or rug. A log of wood on which we laid our parkas, provided a pillow and our pajamas consisted of the clothes on our backs. This was also a welcome insulation against the intense cold after the fire would go out in the small stove during the cold winter nights.

At about six o'clock the next morning, armed with enough food, extra traps, axe and gun, plus flashlight, we would set out along the fur path. Still being dark, we would be directed by shining our flashlights on tree blazes, a strip of bark cut off the trees by an axe on each side, depending on whether we were going from or returning to the tilt. Usually we managed in this way to get to the first trap about dawn.

The trap's location was indicated by a horizontal, instead of a vertical blaze on each tree. Distances between traps were covered with great anticipation. Once we found three bears secured firmly in our bear set. They were fairly young and were quickly killed, skinned and a large portion of the hindquarters was taken to the next tilt to provide a succulent meal that evening. The remainder was put on a crude platform on a pole between trees, well out of the reach of other animals.

In October, the temperatures went well below freezing and so there was no problem presented as far as preservation of the meat was concerned. The only annoyance was evidence of it having provided tasty tidbits at intervals for blue jays or whiskey jacks and some small animals. Spruce partridge were plentiful and it was not unusual to shoot a dozen or more, up to thirty in a day. Other morsels including rabbits were hung in the limbs of trees at a marked spot to be retrieved en route to the next tilt. At times, during the deep snow period, these caches of food were very welcome. One time we shot seven caribou in late November, these were skinned and placed on a large platform built between sturdy trees well out of reach of predators, providing a welcome addition to the diet during the winter.

For most of the fall, until snow made travelling more difficult, Syd and I stayed together building two new tilts and making new blaze marks on trees along the fur path. Trapping for mink and muskrat was usually quite good where the numerous streams entered Grand Lake, until the weather became so inclement that we could not use the canoe. Still, we would venture out from our main tilt to harvest a rich bounty of these valuable pelts. On more than one occasion a fierce bone-chilling snow-squall, accompanied by huge waves, would overtake us when crossing the lake, or between two vantage points for landing. It was touch-and-go and many times we expected to be tossed into the ice-cold waters. When we eventually reached shore, while facing the wind, our clothing would be completely frozen making it almost impossible to stand up. We carried a small balloon silk tent and a metal stove at all times, and in these instances, we selected a sheltered spot, with an abundance of wood, and stayed there until the storm, lasting up to two days, abated. Fried muskrat and partridge supplemented our diet, together with the ever-popular sourdough.

At one time after a canoe trip of four days around the lake, which was five miles long and over two miles wide, a sudden wet snow squall from the northeast sprang up. It hurled us with ever-increasing velocity towards the shore. About ten yards away, a huge wave overturned our canoe, dumping its contents, and two weary trappers, into a frigid bath. Fortunately the water at this point was not deep and we retrieved most of our gear. However, I lost some film of a large lynx we had trapped earlier in the day. Syd had taunted the animal with a long pole to make him show his teeth and extend his paws in our direction while I took several pictures. We dispatched him shortly after. Our clothing was hung on nails driven in the rafters and dried while we went about the task of skinning our catch. I had taken along some of Robert Service's ballads (Cheechako, Rhymes of a Red Cross Man and others) and read them to Syd while he cooked supper.

About the end of November, winter descended in all its fury and bitterness, with sub-zero temperatures prevailing every day accompanied by incessant snowfalls. In two days the huge lake was frozen over and the ice covering became thicker and thicker. For one week, while this weather continued, we stayed in our comfortable main tilt making wooden moulds to stretch and dry our skins, while portioning out supplies to be taken to the other tilts on the path. After a few days, the ice was strong enough to bear our weight and we then chose to go our separate ways. Syd covered the seventy-five to one hundred miles west of the camp and, I, the section east of the lake. The snowshoes or racquets, as they were termed, were the bearpaw type. These made traversing the rough terrain fairly easy compared with the beaver tail or muskeg type, both of which have long tails that invariably hooked into broken branches or fallen trees.

It is an old adage that a man can live without friends, but not without neighbours. I found that being separated from all contact with human beings for long periods of time was indeed frustrating. Many times, the stark fact of being about 150 miles away from Syd Blake and a comparable distance from any habitation drove me to the point of mental panic. What if I were badly cut or injured with no possible source of help for perhaps a week or more? This mental strain was aggravated during a typical day while travelling my section of the trap line.

I had caught very little for two days and decided I would set a few mink traps near the mouth of a large brook. The temperature remained a constant minus thirty-two degrees Fahrenheit. I must have looked an awful sight. My beard and moustache were a frozen mass during the hours of daylight and the ice at the brook's mouth seemed strong enough to bear my weight. I thought the mink must have been travelling under the ice looking for small trout and surfacing along the banks through holes made by the current. The distance between the banks was about sixty feet and having set traps on the near side, I proceeded to cross to the other side. All went well until I had covered about two-thirds of the distance on snowshoes when the ice suddenly gave away.

I felt myself being sucked down by the current and frantically grabbed the ice edges, which gave way with my weight. I immediately flung my rifle toward the opposite bank on safer ice, and I retained my axe which I laid flat hoping it might provide extra support. My snowshoes stubbornly refused to leave my feet, a fact that I was to appreciate, as a moment later, I felt a solid under-footing. I hit a gravel bar, which was fairly wide and extended, I presumed, to the opposite bank. The water here was only about two feet deep allowing me to undo my snowshoes, which I placed on the ice for extra support then, crawled slowly to the opposite bank. Using matches from my water-proof case, I hurriedly built a blazing fire, placed a few boughs upright around the perimeter for the shelter, then divested myself of most of my clothing, hanging it by the fire to dry. Realizing after that, had I not hit the gravel bar, I would have continued into a large pool just below the bar and into extreme difficulty. It is well known that Newfoundlanders swim like rocks.

The temperature at that time of the year hovered around the zero mark and long exposure could cause shock and collapse. How I ever managed to reach safety I do not know, but the old adage "necessity is the mother of invention" was certainly put into practice on that occasion. I used all the miles of my determined nature to get out of my predicament. Having obtained solid ground, I surmised that I had stepped on an area of thin ice under which was an air pocket. Disciplining myself not to panic under any circumstances, and realizing that at times I would be confronted with situations such as this when no help would be available, my whole person thanked the good Lord. Copious amounts of steam arose from my sodden clothing which I dried by rotating pieces in front of the fire. After about an hour, I dressed in my clammy clothing and continued on my way to my cozy tilt, neglecting to examine my traps which, as far as I was concerned, could wait until tomorrow.

Our trap line was about one hundred miles from civilization and total self-reliance was a must. The only other humans encountered were Naskapi Indians roaming the northern section of Labrador, hunting, trapping, and fishing, leading a very nomadic life. Also, there were the Montagnais Indians who roamed the area in Southern Labrador and Quebec from a point where the hamlet of North West River formed a demarcation line to the shores of the Gulf of St. Lawrence. Both areas abounded in caribou and fur. The fishing of char, white fish and suckers was fabulous in summer as well as through the ice in winter. Indians were permitted, by an unwritten agreement, to set their traps within 150 yards of those of a white trapper who, in essence only, owned the trap line. No legal agreement by the Crown at the time was ever signed, but after being handed down by three or four generations of the family, the right of a trapper to continue this practice was recognized by others in the territory.

In summer, the Montagnais Indians would camp on the south bank of the North West River and the Naskapi on a point on the north bank. They rarely mixed, but tolerated each other very well. The Naskapi were the only Indians we encountered in winter. They would come as far south as the Naskapi and Susan River areas to trap small fur-bearing animals. I was of the opinion that they belonged, body and soul, to the Hudson's Bay Company, a company of English adventurers trading into Hudson Bay under a royal charter granted in 1670. Through their many fur-trading posts, they held full sway over immense areas of Canada's north for many years. These Indians were outfitted by the Company each fall and were obligated to bring their furs to them in return. Of course the books were never balanced in the Indian's favour and so the trappers lived and died serfs of the Hudson's Bay Company. An analogous situation existed between the fishermen of the coast and the merchants. They were the victims of a nefarious "truck" system, never getting out of debt to their creditors. Fortunately, the efforts of Grenfell were largely responsible for stamping out this evil, much to the chagrin of the powers that existed and controlled the fishing industry.

As was the practice, I had left a plentiful supply of wood at the tilt and soon had a blazing fire in the small rectangular stove on which I put a kettle of water for tea. The kettle used was made from a lard tin with a piece of stiff wire inserted into two holes, near the top rim, for a handle. It was always black from continued use and too hot to touch, so it was lifted off the stove with a small stick. On the fur path during daytime, it was hung on a stick stuck into the snow and slanted over the fire. When it boiled, a small handful of tea was thrown into the water and allowed to simmer for a moment or two. A little "klim," powdered milk, sugar, and a delicious mug of tea resulted. This is how the trapper's saying "mug up" came about.

When the temperature in the tilt became warm enough, I took off all my clothing and thoroughly dried everything. In the meantime, a rabbit with rice was cooking in the pot. I lay on the soft boughs of the bunk and reflected on how near I had come to drowning, thanking the Almighty for endowing me with such a robust constitution. At that time I weighed 170 pounds, was five-feet, eleven-inches tall, and strong as an ox.

The normal routine was to take the animals from the traps during the daytime, reset them, and get to the next tilt, about twenty miles by dusk. The animals were then hung up on nails driven into the log walls and left to thaw for three or four hours. They were skinned and the pelts were stretched on a wooden mold to dry. At the end of two weeks, I would meet Syd Blake at the main tilt or cabin where the pelts would be carefully packed in a corner, to be taken to the Hudson Bay Post in the spring. Our meeting, every two weeks, was a gala occasion. I would play the mouth organ and read poems of Robert Service through the evening.

Cooking water was obtained by chopping pieces of ice from the lake surface after clearing off the snow. Only on rare occasions when ice was not available did we melt snow to get our water. An inherent belief, on the part of the natives, was that snow water should be avoided, as it would cause illness, especially TB and diarrhea. I concluded that this opinion was held because snow was often contaminated and polluted. It could conceivably cause intestinal disorders, especially if not boiled long enough before use.

Always having deep religious convictions which sustained me in all the vicissitudes of life, my early upbringing and the aura of unselfish devotion, exemplified in the lives of early workers of the Grenfell Mission, was the influence. Practical Christianity was a part of their everyday life and they were led on by the Christian zeal of a true soldier of Christ. I personally heard Dr. Grenfell say that if all hymns, yes even the Bible itself were destroyed, and only one hymn remained, "When I survey the Wondrous Cross," it would suffice to save mankind.

Surrounded by this great wilderness day after day, I came to realize how great and awesome was the universe around us. Northern lights, in all their splendor, formed a transparent curtain of colour against a starry ski in a realm of utter silence at night. Standing outside the tilt, I could actually listen to a kind of subdued breathing of a vast, cold earth at rest. Occasionally a loud cracking of frozen trees, lake ice, or a distant hooting of a snowy owl, were the only sounds to encroach on a world of silence. At times, the soft sighing of a gentle night wind passing through the trees seemed to be telling of the life they were sheltering, knowing that this silence would not last forever.

I carried a small leather-bound book of common prayer, new testament and the hymnal with me, and committed many of their contents to memory. They have comforted me on many occasions when the rough road of life seemed to lead into a world of frustration and despair. Here in the great back of beyond, life seemed so free of worry. Having to be responsible for one's self was challenge enough, not subject to the stresses of living in a dog-eat-dog urban society.

People have often asked how I could relate my religious convictions to that of trapping poor little wild animals. Well, for one thing, I was on the horns of a dilemma. It was fall, I was out of a job, and there was literally no way of getting into the outside world to find one. All the strikes were against me, being the depression years, no roads, airplanes, and the north in the grip of winter which would last until the following June. The only alternative was to embark on a way of life, temporarily, which would at least hold a promise of keeping body and soul together. Killing animals for no other reason than to provide exotic dress for people who could quite easily clad themselves in woolens and synthetic garments seemed a pity. I realized that the fur trade provided wealth and employment for many, but in such an environment shrinking day by day, the denizens of the forest and plains are finding it harder and harder to survive.

Many times while lying on my bunk after a good meal of stewed partridge, rabbit or caribou, I would mull over stories I had heard about Grenfell. He had his forthright manner of shaming wealthy dowagers and people who had fortunately been recipients of a monopoly of this world's goods; goods, whether honestly or otherwise gained, into giving a portion towards the aid of the Mission. If adverse criticism has been leveled at Grenfell for this, one can only recall the rich young man who was challenged to "go sell all that thou hast and give to the poor, take up thy Cross and follow me." The great Master knew that ill gotten wealth could, in the end, cause nothing but sorrow and remorse, the only true joy being found in helping more unfortunates. I realized in the immensity and wonder of nature all around how infinitesimal mankind is, yet "a little lower than the angels." My feeling is that at least eighty percent of people have a genuine desire to help others. Many of those attending Grenfell's lectures in aid of the Mission, did so hoping to do something good and were not unduly hurt by his rather pointed remarks. He thought that a priceless gem should be put to a more useful purpose than to adorn the wearer. In Grenfell's opinion, the harvest was ripe, the labourers few and the time short.

My main task, at this particular time, was to earn enough money to do other things and trapping presented a solution. The winter dragged on, week after week, punctuated by intervals of raging blizzards during which I could not leave the tilt sometimes for two or three days at a time. The swirling snow blowing off lakes and trees formed an impenetrable cloud which, to venture into, would almost certainly result in being lost.

Syd and I entered this forbidden work area about the middle of September. One thing that intrigued me particularly was the great quantity of iron pyrites around the lakeshore. They were often in a layer ten inches deep and I was very sure it must have come from an area in the mountain range. I gathered about five pounds of the rock deposit to have it assayed at a later date. This I did about a year and a half later when I was in Toronto. I phoned Crang & Company, Stock Brokers, telling them of what I considered to be a rich iron deposit in that area of Labrador and asked if they could make an assay. They seemed very eager, took the sample, and from that day on never contacted me despite my many requests for a report. Perhaps I am wrong, but I felt I supplied the "jump-off" information for numerous mining forays into that area and the subsequent establishment of the great mining operations at Wabash and Labrador City, and even towards the largest nickel strike known today at Voisey Bay.

Prior to embarking on my adventure into the bush, I was very privileged to meet Lincoln Elsworth, the Arctic explorer who with a friend Bukman Poole, had made the arduous trip from Seven Islands in the Gulf of St. Lawrence via the Moise River to Hamilton, now Churchill Falls, from there down the Hamilton River to North West River. They shared my accommodation for two nights before catching the mail boat to Rigolet on the Coast, thence by coastal steamer to St. Anthony. Talking with them of their adventures was a most pleasant and memorable experience.

The third week in January saw a cessation of trapping. It was, as Syd remarked, too cold for anything to move. Snow covered the land to a depth of eight to twelve feet and the temperature hovered around fifty to sixty degrees below zero Fahrenheit. What happened to the animals I could not discover, but surmised they must have "holed up" under a blanket of snow living off their fat for the ensuing six weeks when temperatures would moderate. At any rate, trapping came to a complete halt, as there was literally nothing to trap. We had accumulated a considerable number of pelts at our main tilt and decided to spend a week replenishing our stores in the small tilts from our supply at Cape Caribou, before heading to North West River to cash in our skins at the Hudson's Bay Company.

It was a happy day in February when we packed our small toboggans with our catch and our gunnysacks with ample food, then set out for the settlement fifty miles away. We held to the lake surface as much as possible to make snowshoeing easier and after four days arrived to be greeted by friends and relatives. At night en route, we would pitch our balloon silk tent packing snow around its base to a depth of two feet. On the floor we made a comfortable carpet of fir boughs on which to lie, and the small stove soon provided absolute comfort and shelter from the bitter cold outside. We had trapped many kinds of animals including lynx, bear, mink, muskrat, flying squirrels, fox, beaver and ermine. Our total catch amounted to 2,400 dollars, which we considered not too bad for depression times. After paying off our debt for supplies, we received 1,700 dollars, 500 of which was mine to keep. I felt this was ample and as much as I had earned in one year working for the Grenfell Mission.

Sir Wilfred Grenfell had written me previously in September saying "Christ has work for you to do in St. Anthony" and he asked me to get there, if not in the fall, as soon as possible in the spring. I discussed it with Syd and decided that unless I made the trip from North West River to Mary's Harbour before the spring break-up of the rivers and ponds, I would not be able to get to St. Anthony until late June when the coastal steamers would come as far north as Rigolet.

Mary's Harbour on the Labrador side of the Straits of Belle Isle was open for navigation to Flowers Cove on the Newfoundland side much earlier. I therefore decided not to go back trapping for the short spring period but rather to make the trip of some six hundred miles from North West River to Mary's Harbour.

*Nathan Budgell, DVM*

On the morning of March 4, 1932, after having secured a toboggan, sleeping bag, food and a small dog from an Indian family, I prepared to set out on the first leg of my journey. I named my dog "Stump" because of the stump of a tail and short-cropped ears which had been cut off by the Indians as a puppy so that no movement could be seen by caribou when they were stalked on the tundra. Marks of a thong, which had been tied around Stump's nose to prevent him from barking on the hunt, were easily discernable. He was a friendly little chap, quite stocky, well muscled and well able, I figured, to pull a toboggan with a load of about seventy-five pounds. My objective was to walk to Rigolet, a Hudson Bay Post at the mouth of the Hamilton inlet, a distance of 120 miles, and where my uncle George Budgell was Factor Manager. Two nights before, the moon had a golden ring, a portend of possible bad weather, and the night before, snow had begun to fall. On the morning I left it was snowing fairly heavily but with the wind and cold it was dry. Drifting was moderate and little did I think that before nightfall, one of the worst storms of the winter would envelop the whole region and leave about two feet of snow to impede my progress reducing my speed to a snail's pace.

Before actually leaving the hamlet of North West River, I called in on Wilfred Becky who owned two cabins on the north shore of the inlet. One was about ten miles away and the other forty miles. He told me they were stocked with frozen char, seal and other staples, inviting me to help myself. In his cozy kitchen, his wife was working the most beautiful flower into a pair of evening gloves made from deer skin, bleached pure white during the cold Arctic winter. The flower resembled a cornflower and its blue contrasted most beautifully with the pure whiteness of the deerskin. I remarked that I would like to obtain a pair to send to Miss Fellows in England. She produced from a chest another pair of even greater beauty on which was woven a red rose. In addition, she showed me a pair of white matching moccasins trimmed with white rabbit fur. Needless to say, I bought both gloves and moccasins and packed them carefully with the rest of my belongings. Later they were sent to England. Miss Fellows, of course, cherished them and said they were greatly admired by those who saw them.

I left the Beckys' around ten o'clock in the morning hoping to reach his first cabin before dusk. However, the storm had increased in intensity until I could barely see the shoreline. With every step, my snowshoes would sink deeply into the powdery snow and it became almost impossible to pull the toboggan. It was necessary to proceed ahead and to repeat this two or three times before packing the snow firmly enough for the toboggan. Poor Stump was unable to pull and he gave up in despair.

After what seemed like an eternity with dusk beginning to fall, I began to look for the cabin which I felt sure could not be very far away. By this time the storm had abated and the landscape was bathed in silvery moonlight. A pocket thermometer registered twenty-three below zero Fahrenheit, so I decided if I did not find the cabin very soon I'd better consider finding shelter in the dense woods. I was very tired and had not eaten for several hours. I headed for a thick clump of fir trees, and with my axe, hollowed out a crude snow cave about eight feet by four feet and three feet deep. I cut small trees and boughs to make a roof, then built a blazing fire in front. Opening some long sought-after pork and beans Stump and I partook of a meal which any King would have envied under similar circumstances. A strong brew of tea permeated the air, and secured with larded bread we closely settled back enjoying the cheerful fire. Crawling into my sleeping bag about an hour later, feeling very smug in our shelter we soon fell asleep in front of a dying fire around midnight after covering a bare six or seven miles.

What awakened me at four o'clock, I did know, but the wind had started up again and had blown the heat and embers from my fire toward me. My sleeping bag was smoldering along one side so I made a quick exit dragging it into the snow. The outer covering was burned and the fire had just begun to burn the inner lining. Thanking my lucky stars, I proceeded to pack up and head, once again, for the cabin that could not be too far, reaching it at about ten o'clock in the morning. Everything was just as Wilfred had described it, well stocked with a wide bunk and seats made of sawn-off logs about one foot in diameter. I gave Stump a char and cut off a nice chunk of seal meat that was stored in a small lean-to at the rear of the cabin.

Even though snow was falling heavily with the wind increasing, we felt secure and warm, and went outside to get ice from the lake to boil water. I was surprised to see four forms emerging from the drifting snow. They were coming from the south side of the lake and at first I thought them to be from a dog team belonging to one of the trappers. I soon discovered that they were wolves. Stump must have sensed their presence for he ran towards them barking excitedly. They did not, however, deviate from their line of travel and disappeared into the forest about one hundred yards from my cabin. I could see the stark remains of something, probably an ill-fated animal on the ice. It was the first time I had seen wolves in Labrador and after seeing them felt a bit apprehensive.

The wind developed into a gale. For two days I stayed in the warm security of the cabin while all the loose snow which had fallen was swept away from the lake surface into the woods. When I finally resumed my journey, the ice surface was smooth and the going easy. I took ample meat and fish and made good progress without the aid of snowshoes reaching the second cabin just before dark. I covered the twenty to thirty miles in just eight hours! This cabin was not quite as well equipped as the first one, but shelter of any kind was most welcome.

The following day I reached a small tilt that had not been used for some time. It contained a small stove and provided shelter of a type. The Beckys told me that about eighty miles down the inlet I would find a cabin inhabited by a trapper named Harvey Sheppard. I also found several small cabins at intervals of ten to twelve miles used in summer by fishermen. They made their living by fishing and trapping. Just as predicted, I came upon Sheppard's cabin after seven days out of North West River. I had been delayed by bad weather, covering an average of ten to twelve miles daily, which was not the best record.

Sheppard was away, I presume trapping, so I made myself comfortable to await his return. About dusk he appeared with seven partridge, two rabbits and an assortment of small fur-bearing animals. He was quite surprised but pleased to see me and told me that the going from there on to Rigolet could be hazardous for one not acquainted with the route. Twenty miles down, the waters of Lake Milville emptied through a long narrow channel ten miles long and one hundred yards wide into the ocean at Rigolet. Because of numerous eddies, the ice was full of holes between which were thin "bridges" unable to bear a man's weight. He suggested that he accompany me the rest of the way so I heartily agreed. As we neared the narrows on the following day, the vapor danced over the open water like wraiths giving one an eerie feeling. We portaged around dangerous areas then came upon a small log house where an Eskimo, namely Peter Mesher, and family dwelled.

The small children were contentedly sucking seal blubber taken from the large layer of fat surrounding a seal's body. They all wore mukluks made of seal skin and parkas made of caribou skin trimmed with wolf and fox. Their gentle nature and hospitality impressed me so we spent a pleasant night with them continuing the next day to Rigolet, arriving about noon. My uncle, his wife and family, made me very welcome insisting that I have a warm bath and go straight to bed after hearing of my trying trip.

Uncle George suggested that I contact a certain Abe Dyson who was in a village named Cartwright twenty miles away. He was quite certain, that he was going to his home in Black Duck Cove, some sixteen miles from Mary's Harbour. He had a team of nine dogs and would be glad of the company. I could get to Cartwright with the mailman who was expected on the following day.

The mailman arrived early in the morning and left at one o'clock. I bade farewell to Uncle George, leaving Stump with him, much to the delight of the children. They had never seen such an oddity; minus tail, ears and a worn ring around the nose. Stump too seemed happy and I thanked him for providing company for me. He was certainly man's best friend.

At Cartwright I found Dyson who was eager to have me on the 350-mile trip. We loaded the sled or komatik with food, tent and supplies and on March 16 set out on the long trip over muskeg, frozen harbours and lakes and through forests. I was especially fortunate to be with Abe as many of the fishermen moved inland for the winter to the bottom of the Bay where wood, for fuel, was in abundance. Most of the houses were of log construction and located near a brook. Abe knew where everybody lived so we were assured of shelter almost every night even if no one was home. On only two occasions were we obliged to sleep in small cabins used by the mailmen in case of emergency.

One day our team got on the scent of a porcupine. Nothing could restrain them from making a beeline for it. It took us about three hours to remove the quills from their bodies. Another time we arrived at the small hamlet of Bear Cove, consisting of three houses where we found the residents in dire straits. At this time, the effect of the depression was being felt throughout the length and breadth of Newfoundland and Labrador. A "dole" of six cents daily was allowed each individual in a family, barely enough to buy flour, tea and molasses for sweetening. The families had only one quarter of a barrel of flour to last them until the next dole payment in three weeks. They managed to put up some salt codfish and herring and had gathered some partridge and red berries, which were frozen in ice, in the back porch. One mother having no suitable food for her child of six weeks was chewing salt fish to a pulp to extract the salt content. She then took it out of her mouth and fed it to the child.

The houses, if they could be called such, consisted of one large room with a rough wooden plank floor. At one end was a wood-burning stove and a kitchen table with benches. At the other end, two wide bunks were built next to the wall and covered with marsh grass for mattresses with hand-made patchwork quilts for covering. The men occupied the upper bunk, sleeping often three or four in a row. The women slept in the lower bunk. The house in which I stayed had a lean-to forming an extra room in which the wife of one member, heavy with child, slept. There were no shingles or tarpaper available, the roof was covered with sod to a depth of six inches. The sound emanating from the lean-to bedroom caused me to fear that I might be asked to assist a probably unwanted individual into this adverse environment.

As expected, I had made myself comfortable in my sleeping bag when, at about four in the morning, loud anguished cries awakened me. It was at once apparent that assistance was needed for the woman so I prepared the necessary hot water, clothes and soap. A fortunate find was a bath towel that would be suitable for wrapping the infant in. The baby's head was just beginning to protrude but seemed to be jammed. It would not exit in spite of constant pressure. Obtaining a piece of stout rope, I made a sling for each of the mother's legs elevating them by tying them to an overhead rafter. I then wrapped a clean sheet around the abdomen applying tension, thus exerting more pressure.

The coal-oil lantern, hanging overhead on a nail provided an eerie light to this macabre scene. Using lard as a lubricant, I managed to manipulate the head, then the shoulders out, the rest followed quickly. I tied the naval cord with thread, cleared out the phlegm in the mouth with my index finger, then, holding it by the feet patted its rear and back. Loud yells burst forth and soon a beautiful baby boy was held in a towel by a fond aunt by the warm stove.

The mother was attended to by one of the elder girls, about fourteen years of age. She made her mother as comfortable as possible with the meager homemade dressings and coverings. By noon, mother and son were doing very well. I dreaded to think what might have happened had serious complications developed with no doctor or nurse within fifty or sixty miles.

The following day being Sunday, I was asked to hold a short church service accompanied by my harmonica. We sang many of the old favorites: "We Have an Anchor," "Blessed Assurance" and "Rock of Ages." We gave thanks for the very fact of life itself and asked Him to guide us through the difficult period of the depression and on to better times. All these simple people really wanted was to be free of want from those things needed merely to sustain life. I could think of no better way to celebrate the joyous occasion of a baby boy's birth, than to offer most of the remainder of my supplies: pork and beans, corned beef, canned peaches and one canned ham. Their gratitude was such that in retrospect, I do not think that I have ever experienced such happiness at a "Feast."

Bear Cove Hamlet was situated at the mouth of a small river and I noticed holes in several places where water had eroded the ice from underneath. I inquired if anybody had thought of testing these holes for trout and was rather surprised to be told that trout could not be caught through the ice until May.

I decided to try and wonder-of-wonders my first attempt produced a lovely fish weighing over one pound. The people did not appear enthused at the prospect of a welcome supplement to their diet and I discovered this was due to my having violated the eighth, ninth and tenth commandments, a Cardinal Sin in the estimation of these God-fearing people. I tried to explain that God, the giver of life, would not look unkindly on such an act and that His Son even gathered corn on Sunday to feed the fold. They reluctantly agreed but then became quite convinced when within the space of an hour, they had caught thirty-eight beautiful trout that were totally consumed at supper that night.

The next morning it was reported that a polar bear had landed from floe ice on a point two miles from the settlement. Three men went in pursuit, in anticipation, of a plentiful supply of fresh meat, but returned in four hours after an unsuccessful hunt. Their effort was not without reward, however, for they killed sixteen sea ducks among some two hundred trapped in the small area of open water near the shore.

Quite a number of seals was taken during the spring months and the men told of two brothers who were killed three years previously while seal hunting. They lay down behind an ice hummock to watch for seals emerging from their holes in the ice and were mistaken for seals by another hunting party. The incident brought great sadness to the hamlet and seemed very fresh in their memories. When I left the following morning, I felt gratified to think that I had at least alleviated some of the monotony and was particularly pleased, having brought another Labrador citizen into the world.

*A Newfoundland Son*

At all the villages between Cartwright and Mary's Harbour we encountered genuine friendship and hospitality from every person. Those more fortunate than others shared their food and clothing with those in need. Their consideration for children was overwhelming, making very sure that the needs of the little ones should come first. It seems sad that these simple hard-working men and women wresting their living from the icy waters of the Labrador current, constantly in danger on the raging waters, providing food for the tables of the outside world, should be so impoverished, through no fault of their own.

The Great Depression was largely the result of greed and avarice on the part of people eager to amass great wealth at the expense of unfortunates. Many invested their life savings in worthless ventures at the behest of promoters with glib tongues. Little did I realize the implications or become emotionally involved in the reactions of those who were now feeling the impact of want and frustration. However, I had not long to wait because in a few short months I too was one of those "riding the rods" out West vainly searching for a job of any description.

We continued on to St. Michael's Bay where during the crossing we came to a near catastrophe. The ice was beginning to become mushy due to the increasing heat of the sun and erosion underneath by warming ocean currents. We stopped at a small tilt on the north shore of the Bay for the night on the three-day trip from Bear Cove. Due to the swelling rivers and brooks we often had to circumvent them at their mouths, the detour at times being several miles. All of the dog food had been used and none could be had until we reached St. Michael's, a hamlet of fifteen souls on the other side of the Bay. Abe seemed to be a bit apprehensive over the attitude of hungry dogs obliged to haul our sled over what might prove to be the most difficult part of our journey.

A heavy snowstorm started during the night and in the morning, our nine dogs appeared as small mounds of snow completely covered to a depth of two feet. I cautiously approached one mound and discovered a small hole leading to the surface where I surmised the nose to be. A gentle nudge with the foot and a very sleepy dog appeared out of the snow blanket shaking himself vigorously. Together with the others, he had been completely insulated from the cold and storm. Our only real worry was that we had no dog food, (seal, corn meal or blubber).

In spite of the density of the falling snow and wind, we decided to cross the Bay ice, although treacherous, rather than make a long detour around. Abe remarked that a small island was located about half way across and although we could not see it in the dense snow, he assured me that the lead dog named "Luke" had been across before and would lead us to it. We could plainly hear the crashing and grinding of the floe ice and I must confess it sent a chill up my spine. Abe, however, seemed unperturbed and we set off in the swirling snow.

*Nathan Budgell, DVM*

We took turns walking in front of the team on snowshoes to pack the snow that, by this time, had attained a depth of about three feet. After one hundred yards or so, the one in front would go to the rear until Luke had sniffed his way once again in the direction of the island. Several times Abe insisted that the land resided to the right or left but Luke, by some uncanny instinct, would veer off in another direction until what seemed like an eternity, the island loomed ahead.

It had taken three hours to cover four miles. Finding a valley at the cliff edge, we were soon in a wooded area temporarily sheltered from the elements. A blazing fire, mug of hot tea with bread heightened our spirits and we climbed to the top of the hill to get our bearings. Visibility was almost nil but Abe selected a point on the far side where we could start out again. The ice seemed firm enough except for soft spots, which were full of water. The poor dogs found these very trying having to work much harder on empty stomachs. Sometimes the water was three or four feet deep and we prayed that it did not extend down to the Bays bottom. Six miles were still to be covered which would seem like a hundred. Walking in front was almost impossibility as our snowshoes sank in slush at every step. We decided to sit on the sled, extending one leg over the side, pushing as best we could to help the dogs.

Fortunately, the storm abated somewhat enabling us to see the opposite shore as a long blur, four miles away. After passing over another mile of slush, the surface appeared firmer. Abe sprang off the komatik, or sled while holding onto the nose of the runners to ease his weight. He immediately broke through sinking to his waist in cold, icy water. The ice could bear the weight of individual dogs, but not that of a man. He held onto the sled and hauled himself aboard. It was no use complaining as we were in a predicament and to carry on was the only way out. The dogs were almost too tired to haul, looking back at us as if to emphasize the point.

Stopping for a few minutes we contemplated a detour, but found nothing that looked safer. We decided that one of us would have to don snowshoes and walk ahead to lighten the load. I insisted on taking the job as Abe was, by this time, shivering in wet clothes. All went well, and the sight of me in front gave courage to the poor dogs that strained to keep up. Twice I sank to my knees in wet slush but eventually reached the ballycaters (local name for ice pinnacles near the shore) and struggled on to the safety of solid land. How grateful and relieved we were. Three miles further, two drenched and half-frozen humans with exhausted dogs knocked on the door of a merchant who upon seeing these two spectacles, caused him, to almost lose his false teeth. It was not long before we had a dry change of clothing and lots of food for our dogs, which then curled up contentedly for over twenty-four hours.

The conversation centered around how lucky we were to be alive and safe, as travel over the route we had taken had been abandoned three weeks earlier. They were surprised that we had not drowned in one of the water holes, or perished from the cold. After a hearty supper of duck and vegetables, we bedded down for a good night's sleep.

I was sorry the next day to have to say goodbye to my good friend, Abe Dyson, as he left with his team. I found him to be a most unusual, and if the term can be fittingly used, loveable character. He never became unduly perturbed in the face of danger and had an inherent sense of humour.

One story, which I enjoyed very much, was about a woman living in a small community on the coast who kept two or three cows. She would make butter from surplus milk and sell it to the neighbours. However, wrapping material was scarce, and with the cows, she also kept two pet dogs that continually shed hair on the kitchen floor. A customer called in for butter one day and she placed a large piece on the kitchen table, preparatory to cutting off a portion. During the operation, the piece slipped on to the floor. She immediately picked it up and offered it to the client asking if he would like it wrapped. He remarked "oh, no ma'am, I'll drag it home by the hair."

Another story during the war before Newfoundland was part of Canada was about a German who came to shore from a submarine in Newfoundland to buy supplies. His English was very good and did not think he was detected. A piece of meat fell to the floor and again became full of hair. He looked at the meat and remarked "it's full of hair." The shop keeper said, "dat's alright bi; a little bit of the air of da dog dat's going bite and eat ye all up."

At St. Michael's, I met a man who was going to St. Mary's Harbour for his monthly dole supply. He had a team of three dogs and a small keg strapped to the rear of his komatik to be filled with molasses. A rectangular box, about two by five feet and one foot deep, went along to receive the remainder of food consisting of flour, tea, fat back pork and other staples.

I joined him without question and found the terrain between St. Michael's and Mary's Harbour to be very hilly and the route rather treacherous. It was difficult to control the sled on the icy surface of the barrens, especially when going downhill. I was designated to sit on a rope, stretched between the nose of the sled runners and plant my feet firmly on the ground to act as a drag. My companion knelt on the back of the sled, and used a stick, which he inserted between the bar holding the two runners together contacting the surface underneath, helping further to slow the downhill speed. At one point, the stick broke, and in spite of desperate efforts on my part to maneuver the sled, it hit a very frozen piece of earth, stopping abruptly. Everything came to a complete standstill. My friend was badly bruised on the ribs, which hit the molasses keg. He evidenced intense pain and I feared he might have ruptured the liver or lung, so I laid him in the box then proceeded as quickly as possible to the nursing station at St. Mary's Harbour.

That hill proved to be the last difficult hurdle, and, a competent nurse at the station attended to his wounds. He insisted that I pay him one hundred dollars for having supposedly caused the injury through carelessness, but viewing this demand as ridiculous, I refused. There were no lawyers or courthouses within three hundred miles, and I felt secure that I would not be delayed by a senseless charge. I give him ten dollars, a fortune at that time, and I never heard anything afterward.

The nursing station at St. Mary's was established after the disastrous fire that destroyed the hospital at Battle Harbour. St. Mary's River empties into St. Louis Bay, well protected and wooded and totally different from Battle Harbour. Falls on the river about two miles up from its mouth are very picturesque and great fishing can be had both above and below them. It would be three weeks or so before the first boat would arrive to take me across to Flowers Cove to another Grenfell station via the narrow straits of Belle Isle, separating Labrador and Newfoundland.

I decided to use some dogs, which were available to haul earth from a source over a mile away. This was to be used to make a vegetable garden. The station kept one cow, which had arrived in calf, on the last boat in October. She was due in late May or June and had left a copious hill of fertilizer to mix with the soil. By the time the coastal steamer "Sagona" arrived in late May, I proudly viewed a garden measuring sixty by thirty-five feet seeded with cabbage, carrots, beets, turnips and lettuce. Dr. Moret, the doctor in charge, told me later in St. Anthony that he harvested some cabbages weighing between fifteen and twenty pounds. Turnips did very well and lasted in the protection of a sod covered roof house or (root cellar) well into the winter.

On June 3, I embarked on the coastal steamer "Sagona," belonging to the Newfoundland Steam Ships, a government operated service bringing supplies, including mail and passengers, to the outports. Any settlement removed from highway or railway contact with St. John's, the capital city, was designated an outport. It was indeed a welcome occasion, after a long winter completely isolated from larger centers, to hear the siren of the first boat nosing her way through the innumerable icebergs and floes that still dotted the oceans and harbours.

The "Sagona" was a veteran sheathed with copper and greenhart to combat ice conditions. She would push her way across the Straits in the direction of Flower's Cove arriving after twelve hours of ice hammering in the snug harbour. Navigation on the west coast opened earlier than on the east due to its being protected from the large ice masses carried south by the Labrador Current, finally meeting their doom in the warm shallow waters of the Grand Banks. The great tragedy of the Titanic occurred shortly before my birth, in 1912, after colliding with one of these huge masses of ice.

Every inhabitant of Flower's Cove seemed to be on the wharf when we tied up. I went to the parsonage where Parson Richards lived, a well-loved and devoted Church of England Minister, and a great friend of Sir Wilfred Grenfell.

His work among the fisher folk in that area will long be remembered. He invited me to stay until I could set out on foot for St. Anthony some 150 miles away going over extremely rough terrain via the coastline. There was a trail over land used in the winter by dog teams, leading through forest and muskeg; almost impossible to traverse in spring. Also along the coast were small fishing hamlets in which one could find shelter at night.

Taking leave of my kind host, I set out two days later for Eddy's Cove, a prosperous village, stopping en route at Savage Cove and then Eddy's Cove West for the night. At Eddy's Cove West I was fortunate to join a group of men from Eddy's Cove who were visiting by boat. I enjoyed comfortable transit along a particularly difficult length of coastline and spent the night with the very hospitable family of Isaac White. They were most kind and said that in two days a motorboat would be going to Big Brook some twenty miles further on. There I could stay with relatives, the McLeans and prepare for the journey to Cape Norman, which most certainly would have to be made on foot.

In spite of my insistence that I pay something from my rather meager funds for all their kindness, every person with whom I stayed refused to accept anything. In spite of it being in the middle of the Great Depression; their generosity shone. I could only thank them and being one of their kin could readily understand. Hospitality was almost a vice nurtured by having to help each other in the everyday challenge of wresting a living from the sea.

Big Brook proved to be a small fishing community of nine families on the "Strait" shore at the entrance of the Straits of Belle Isle and being kin I was made very welcome. Large icebergs were everywhere having grounded on the shallow waters where they were being pounded by huge waves breaking them up. The noise of thousands of tons splitting off from the huge mass reverberated like thunder day and night. One particularly large one was aground just off the eastern tip of Belle Isle and in my estimation measured several hundred yards in length and about six hundred feet high.

The reader may wonder why I was compelled to take such a circuitous route to reach St. Anthony. It must be remembered that there were no roads, railways or airplanes. An occasional plane did find its way into the north, but in 1933, travel as we know it today was in its infancy. Nungesser and Coli, two intrepid French aviators, had been lost only a short while before, while trying to fly from Europe to North America and the crew of the Bremen narrowly escaped death when they were forced to crash land on Greely Island off the Labrador Coast. Coastal steamers could not operate safely on the east coast of Newfoundland until mid-June because of the ice and in any case, did not service the area between Flower's Cove and Cape Norman.

Sir Wilfred asked me to get to St. Anthony as soon as possible in the spring to help with the preparation and planting of the gardens. There remained no alternative but to cross the Straits on the earliest steamer and then to walk, or hitch rides with fishermen in their small boats. After a day's stop-over in Big Brook, I bade farewell to the McLeans with a wish that we might have the pleasure of meeting again in the future.

Travelling lightly, with about fifty pounds on my back, axe and rifle, I covered the twenty-two miles to Cook's Harbour in record time enjoying the landscape which, with its large boulders and barrenness, resembled a moonscape. It was devoid of trees and small water holes dotted the area in which thousands of waterfowl were resting on their journey north. I presumed that glacial action, eons ago must have created this unusual affect.

At Cook's Harbour, I went to the residence of Isaac Warren, a very successful fisherman. With his two sons and four hired hands, he worked the trap fishery industry in cod rich waters. The "trap" consisted of four walls of net with a "door" cleverly designed so that the fish swimming off shore, in pursuit of the myriad of caplin, would be directed into the enclosure and trapped. Boats would then surround the net and pull on ropes closing the bottom and door, thus capturing the cod in a huge enclosed restraint. Pulling on the ropes reduced the size of the space and as the fish were near the surface, the water would literally boil with the seething mass. A dip net rather like the conventional fisherman's net, but having a much longer handle was then employed to transfer the catch to the boats.

The cod were taken ashore by means of a hay pitchfork, pitched up on a platform or stage made of small trees and planks. At two or three places in this structure were square holes under a splitting table to allow the offal to be dumped into the water. On the table, women set about the work of removing the fish heads and entrails. The fish were then placed in wheelbarrows and taken to the salting shed. Here they were laid in rows of about three feet deep, with salt placed between each row for curing. Adjoining the shed were fish flakes made of poles placed horizontally and spaced to allow air to circulate freely. After a period of curing, they were laid to dry and sun cure on these flakes. This was how the term "sun cured" came into use for many years.

Even before refrigeration came into use, salt cod graced the tables of many countries, including those of the Caribbean, Portugal and Spain, where religious ritual dictated that fish be eaten on Friday. At that time, cod sold for half a cent a pound green, and two cents dried, barely enough to sustain a family through the winter unless a great quantity was marketed. The trapped catch on some days would amount to over a hundred quintals, or 112 pounds. The cod season did not last long after the caplin had spawned, maybe six weeks at the most, after that they were taken by jigging. A man adept at jigging could catch around five quintals a day.

I stayed with the Warrens and helped with the fishery while waiting for the coastal steamer. Once or twice, on windy days, we would go up the Bay to attend the gardens, which had been set prior to the fishery. In the sheltered inlet the soil was good, having been cultivated for many years. The turnips, potatoes and cabbage, were well fertilized with kelp and caplin, and were growing beautifully. The odour was not any more unpleasant than that of farmyard manure, and no insecticides were used.

At the end of three weeks, a schooner owned by a Captain Vallence of Grand Bank came into Cook's Harbour with a load of coal destined for the government lighthouse on Cape Norman. It was a small vessel of some eighty tons with mainsail, foresail, topsail and three jibs. The good Captain advised that the coastal steamer would not be in that vicinity for about two weeks, having to replenish depleted supplies, after the long freeze-up in the settlements along the east coast. He suggested that I act as a deck hand, along with his crew of three, as far as the Cape and back to Griquet, which was overland, about twenty-five miles from St. Anthony. He would leave me there and it would take me only a day's walk to reach my ultimate destination.

I spent eight days on the small craft avoiding icebergs, passing in and out of narrow, sheltered inlets until we reached Cape Norman, unloaded, and proceeded to Griquet. My main job was to trim the Jumbo, a large jib sheet that had to be manually hauled every time the schooner swung into the wind on the attack. How many times I heard the command "Trim the Jumbo," I cannot remember, but it must have been hundreds.

Arriving at Griquet we tied up at the wharf of Esaw Hillier, a local fish merchant with whom I stayed over night. Both Esaw and his wife were most charming and hospitable, as were their daughters, Evelyn and Sybil. I fell completely in love with Evelyn. Her long black hair and deep blue eyes made a beautiful contrast with her fair complexion.

Across the harbour was the Church of England in which services were held every three weeks by a travelling parson visiting area settlements in rotation. Esaw told me that once the Bishop of Newfoundland came into Griquet quite unexpectedly one summer's day. An old lady, the pillar of the church, was responsible for having everything ready, even to chopping wood for the fire to make his cup of tea. She was diligently, and with great concentration, splitting the small chunks of wood, completely oblivious of the fact that the Bishop was even then approaching her on a small footpath leading from the wharf. He hailed her with a loud "Well you're splitting her up ma'am." Without turning around she said quite innocently, "Well don't keep a talkin' bi, git de udder axe and lend a and, weeze gittin' ready for da Bishop". It was said that the Bishop would send a murmur of laughter through his congregations on many occasions when relating the experience.

The next day the Hilliers described the overland route I would have to follow to St. Anthony. I felt downhearted at having to say good-bye to Evelyn. However, tempus fugit and we must meet our needs trying to keep pace in our fleeting span of life. I set out with a sandwich and an apple for what I reckoned would be a pleasant hike of just over twenty miles. The long days of June provided plenty of light and I followed the old telegraph line on and on.

After many hours, I feared something had gone awry as two sets of lines suddenly presented a conundrum. I chose to take the one leading to the right, and in so doing, got myself in a sorry fix. Keeping on and on over brooks, bogs and woods, I finally decided I must have taken the wrong turn. Climbing a small hill, I could see a vast expanse of water about two miles away, and at the same time discovered that the poles were bereft of wires. Undaunted, I proceeded until I came to the sandy shores of what I concluded to be Hare Bay, a large area of water on the north-east coast of the Great Northern Peninsula.

As dusk was beginning to settle at this time and my food gone, I decided the first requirement was shelter for the night. I was fortunate to find an abandoned cabin with a roof in fair condition, used at some time by fishermen or trappers. Doors and windows were missing and the floor was just plain earth. After being inside for a few minutes I found myself surrounded by hordes of mosquitoes. My only recourse was to dig, with the aid of my axe, a hole in the floor near the door. Here I made a fire hoping the draft from the opening would carry the smoke either through the roof, in which were several open seams, or through the open windows. It worked, and after the ash was bright red I packed on moss which was easily available to make a smudge. I retreated to the farthest point from the smoke and began to explore the area for any possible food.

On a small shelf in one corner I found several caplin thoroughly dried, but very old and stale. In an empty flour barrel was about one quarter inch of dried, caked flour. I turned the barrel upside down, dislodged the contents and skimmed up as much as possible of the revolting affair. This curbed the hunger I was feeling. I sat on the floor, with my back to the wall, and slept fitfully through the long, dark night. My smudge fire proved very effective in keeping the mosquitoes away.

At daybreak I took stock of my situation and decided the best procedure would be to retrace my steps to a fishing village called St. Leonard's, eight miles from Griquet. By this time I was very hungry and still weary. However, I made fairly good progress until about four miles from St. Leonards when I was forced to sit down and rest every few hundred yards. On reaching the village, I went to the Bursey Store, owned by the local merchant and was made most welcome. Mrs. Bursey was very concerned with my appearance. She gave me some warm bread and milk, saying I shouldn't eat a heavy meal until later. I enjoyed a warm bath and later in the evening dined heartily. They heard that the coastal steamer "Prospero" was expected in two days so on their insistence, I stayed until its arrival. In the meantime, I availed myself of the opportunity to visit the Hilliers by boat, spending a pleasant two hours with Evelyn, the object of my infatuation. We promised to write each other often. I returned to St. Leonards, and on the next day boarded the steamer for St. Anthony.

The Hilliers had informed Dr. Charles Curtis, Medical Superintendent of the Grenfell Mission by wire, that I would arrive that day. When the ship reached the pier, he spotted me and seemed in a state of great agitation. Having received the telegraph from Esaw Hillier, he expected me to arrive in St. Anthony by three days hence at about seven or eight o'clock that same evening. He sent out a search party, scouring the white and grebes nest hills area to within eight miles of Griquet. His relief in knowing I was safe was overwhelming. He embraced me warmly and invited me to stay with him for a day or two until I felt rested.

Dr. Curtis was, as a rule, quite undemonstrative and unemotional, so I felt honoured indeed to have been the recipient of such genuine concern. As far as I could observe, Dr. Curtis never attended church or joined in evening prayers or hymns. These were a part of hospital routine just before lights out, and yet "he went about doing good" as was said of the Master. He shepherded the work of the Mission in its every phase, tending the sick, encouraging farming, fostering higher education, as well as taking personal interest in problems of all the citizens of St. Anthony.

As I have said, he was undemonstrative but one felt all was well with this isolated outpost of Christian endeavor under his guidance. He eventually married Harriett Houghteling; active in higher education and after whom the Harriett Houghteling High School was named. Often when the good doctor was needed urgently at the hospital, he could be found diligently hand-milking a cow in the barn, or perhaps transplanting cabbages in the Mission gardens. He was truly a doer of the word.

A few days after arriving in St. Anthony, the S.S. Strathcona came into port, bringing Sir Wilfred Grenfell on his annual visit to the coast. I met him quite by accident the following day. He was sitting on an oil drum all alone near the wharf. We engaged in a long conversation centering on the reason for my leaving North West River. He wanted to know all about every family from Rigolet to Mary's Harbour. Darkness was settling over the harbour when he decided it was time to eat. He invited me to dine with him at his residence. It was there that I saw the brass plaque he had placed on the wall in the hall. It read "In memory of three noble dogs, Watch, Moody and Spy whose lives were given for mine on the ice, April 21, 1908."

I had occasion to talk with him several times during the ensuing summer. A group of us decided to start a small newspaper, which we called "The Northern Lights." Grenfell helped us procure a printing press that, though rather antiquated, served its purpose well. The paper was flourishing when I left St. Anthony in 1933, and continued to do so for many years after. I was informed that it ceased publication during the early years of World War II.

I found comfortable board and lodging with Mr. and Mrs. Wilfred Mesher who had a dwelling quite near the gardens and farms. The working day at that time began at seven o'clock and ended at six o'clock, with an hour off for lunch.

The pay was one dollar and eighty cents a day until money became so scarce that labour was paid for with a voucher at the Capitals Spot Cash Store, operated by the Grenfell Association for ten dollars a week. My board and lodging were paid for and in addition I consumed six dollars worth of groceries weekly, leaving three dollars for personal needs. Absolutely no cash was available and I could not find enough money to buy a stamp. Keeping in constant touch with Miss Fellows was important and I explained my predicament to Dr. Curtis. He extended me a small additional cash allowance but advised that it might be better if I could possibly find a way to get to Canada.

In September of 1933, the cruise ship "New Northland" visited St. Anthony and was returning to Montreal later the same month. I wired my sister Bertha in Toronto, advising that I would be arriving there in due course. All of the accommodation was booked, but the purser found me small, cramped, but comfortable quarters on board.

It was with heavy heart that I watched the familiar sites of the town recede as we steamed out of the harbour. En route to Montreal, we sailed up the beautiful Saguenay River, past Capes Trinity and Eternity ablaze with early autumn colours, and then up the mighty St. Lawrence to disembark at Montreal.

An old school chum of mine who had a permanent job with the Grenfell Mission had given me twenty dollars, in addition to my fare. Hailing a taxi I was taken to the railway station to await a train to Toronto. I forgot just how long I waited but it seemed interminable. Inquiring at the bookstand, I was told that the best current reading material, the book of the year, was "Anthony Adverse." I bought it for about three dollars, all seven hundred pages in very fine print, a tome, which proved to be the most uninteresting piece of literature I ever had occasion to read. The fare was nine dollars and I was relieved when the train finally pulled out.

On the way a well-dressed gentleman asked me if I preferred going on a C.N.R. or C.P.R. train, and I was at a loss to express an opinion, not having traveled more than ten miles on either. Sitting in the station in Montreal, I found it very difficult to understand why everybody seemed to be rushing here and there, yet going nowhere. Not that I am trying to minimize the importance of our ant-like movements as conducive to progress, but having come from an area where mañana, as in the South, was the order of the day, I could not adjust myself to the incessant rush. In Newfoundland and Labrador everyone stopped to say "good-day" or "hello," but not so with the automated mass of humanity in the railway station.

In Toronto, I found it to be the same, and thought I had better get into the stream, if success were to be attained. My sister lived in a modest three-bedroom house at 86 Rowntree Avenue, with her husband Stewart, many years her senior. He worked at Acme Screw & Gear on Weston Road, and Sis worked a local dry cleaners as floor lady. The sojourn with my relatives was short, but I outlined to them what I had in mind.

# CHAPTER IX - THE DEPRESSION YEARS

While on the New Northland, I met Mrs. Milton Seeley, of Wonalancet, New Hampshire. She and her husband owned and operated the Chinook Kennels, training huskies for the Byrd expedition. They also sold dogs to various sled-racing fanciers in the New England States. My experiences in Labrador and Newfoundland were such that Mrs. Seeley contacted Admiral Richard Evelyn Byrd, arctic explorer, who was about to embark from Boston in the "Jacob Rupert" with a view to taking me as a driver for his dog team. He seemed very eager and asked that I report, as soon as possible, to him. I was racing against time as the ship was due to leave in two days. I hurriedly packed, caught a bus via Buffalo, New York, where the immigration authorities held me up on technicalities for two days. Naturally, the expedition was carried on without me.

I continued on and spent the winter training and racing dogs for Admiral Bird at the Chinook Kennels and at carnivals under the auspices of the New England Sled Dog Club. Avid supporters of this sport were: Mosley Taylor of the Boston Globe, and Major Erland Goyette of Manchester, New Hampshire Linen Mills. We held a reception and ball at the arena in Boston and among the notables who attended was, Leonard Seppala, of Alaska fame.

I had the distinction of being the youngest driver with a new team of dogs to win the New Hampshire Derby with Fox Film Services recording the event. It was shown all over the continent in newsreels and many fans wrote expressing interest in the event. I had hoped to continue on the following year but could not, in any way, get an extension of my temporary visa. This was due to the scarcity of jobs for the average American citizen. All efforts by Mr. Seeley, who journeyed to Newport to see the immigration officials on my behalf, were fruitless. So in early April, 1934, I returned to Toronto.

My sister had, during my absence, opened a small dry cleaning business on College Street. She called it Osmond Cleaners. The depression was being felt everywhere. In the States I had seen hundreds of young men at C.C.C. (Civilian Conservation Camps), initiated by President Roosevelt to keep crime in check by providing food, shelter and useful labour. They did an excellent job of clearing and improving forestlands, creating parks, building bridges and other infrastructure projects. The T.V.A. (Tennessee Valley Authority) was created to build the Norris Dam, improving the whole agricultural and industrial potential of the Tennessee Valley. In Toronto, long lines of men formed at the Fred Victor Mission on Jarvis Street for their daily ration of soup and then slept at the Salvation Army for a pittance. If any of them were totally broke, they simply did not pay. Discontent was rife, there was no Unemployment Insurance, and Welfare hardly provided enough to keep body and soul together.

Camps were established in some northern areas and men were located in them to cut pulpwood for ten dollars a month plus board. A feeling of utter frustration pervaded every facet of society. Men by the thousands invaded the west for farm work that paid ten dollars a week plus board, for a fourteen-hour day, six days straight. They got out west by any available means, usually taking the ferry from Port McNichol to Fort William, then riding the rods in empty box cars to Winnipeg and points further on. Regina was a rallying point where farmers often hired men.

I decided to try my luck also, and joining company with three companions, set out for Port McNichol. On reaching Fort William, we scouted the rail yards for an empty boxcar; there were many of these returning for grain. Fort William and Port Arthur were twin cities through which much of the grain from the great western plains was stored in huge elevators, then shipped by water to England and Europe. It was a scene of great activity and railway police or "bulls" were seen everywhere. Their job was to see that vagrants, as we were classed, did not board the empty cars. For some unexplained reason, all the doors on the cars were left open about three feet. The reason I assumed to be, for allowing the interior to be air dried after being washed down. These were invariably left open when the train pulled out, and provided ready access to a box car, even while the train was moving out of the yard. A mad last-minute scramble ensued from every hiding point in the yard and a goodly number of unwanted transients managed a free ride to Winnipeg.

At Kenora nobody inspected the boxcars, but at Winnipeg several "bulls" appeared. Nothing was done, as it would have been impossible to jail all the vagrants, and there was no use imposing a fine as none had the wherewithal to pay. I guess the powers-to-be agreed to accept the lesser of the two evils, and take the attitude that there was really nothing fundamentally wrong with people seeking access to work by whatever means. We carried out our ablutions in the washrooms at the stations and then scouted around for handouts from small stores on the Portage Avenue, Main Street area. People were usually well disposed toward us.

From Winnipeg on, the going was not too bad and I eventually stopped off at Newdale, Manitoba, near the Saskatchewan border, on the farm of Robert Irvine. I stayed there with his wife and family and I have never had the pleasure of meeting lovelier people. He had a herd of Red Poll beef, and farmed with his sons, a half section of land. My agricultural training in England stood me in good stead, so I was given work on the farm for the summer at ten dollars per week plus board. Meals were good, the work hard and long, but I was in fit condition to take it. I ploughed, seeded and harvested root and grain crops. By September, I had saved enough to pay my train fare back to Toronto. Mr. Irvine said he could keep me all winter but could not afford to pay me. In view of this, I thought it best to go to a city where more opportunity might be available.

Arriving once again at my sister's on September 24, I found that she had rented her house on Rowntree Avenue and had moved into two rooms behind her cleaning store. She bought a 1932 Studebaker Sedan, second hand, complete with polished paneling and curtains, having fringe and tassels to protect the passengers from the prying eyes of the public. She was using it to pick up and deliver cleaning for her customers. I thought the curtains were very appropriate for hiding from view the garments inside. I drove this beautiful and almost wholly hand-made vehicle, thither and yon, to every part of Toronto.

The process of cleaning rather amused me. My sister had very little money with which to start a business, so decided to cut the procedure employed by large firms, which was to immerse the cleaning in a large drum containing cleaning fluid, then spinning it until all the dirt was extracted. She duplicated this in a more primitive manner by immersing the cleaning in a metal container holding about two gallons of fluid. Using a plunger, as is used to unplug toilets, she would extract the dirt manually.

It seemed to work satisfactorily, except on one occasion, when a lady presented a Karakul Persian lamb coat for cleaning. Apparently the wool used for its manufacture was twisted into a long rope about one quarter of an inch thick, then sewn in a zigzag pattern on the underneath fabric. The plunging proved to be too much for the thread, so to our dismay, when we pulled the coat out of the solution, only the fabric appeared, leaving a large saddened mass of wool in the container. We were both heart-broken as it was a valuable coat. What to do! My sister and I spent three whole nights, until six o'clock in the morning, sewing back what we could to salvage the wool. She phoned the lady saying that the coat was very dirty and required special treatment. Special all right! However, when the lady returned, she was simply thrilled with the appearance and the quality of our work and said she had never seen such a fine job. There was a considerable amount of wool left over from our dilemma, but the lady seemed not to notice. We collected the huge sum of six and half-dollars for all our labour.

The months wore on and in December, another calamity hit us. While driving the Studebaker up a steep incline off Davenport Road, the transmission gave out. I had to back down on the level roadway into a small alcove on the side of the road. The cost of the transmission and repairs was prohibitive, amounting to some 130 dollars, so we decided to let the garage haul it away. The garage bought it for seventy dollars so thereafter; I delivered by streetcar, or on foot, all over the city.

The depression seemed to be at its worst during 1933 and 1934. Bread lines became longer and the mood of the people, decidedly more somber and depressing. In the Canadian West, the fiery young politicians: C.C.F. Tommy Douglas, together with Woodworth and Coldwell, were making vociferous appeals to the government to create public works. Mr. Douglas appealed to Finance Minister, Mr. Dunning, to allocate a mere ten million dollars for this purpose. He was told that "money doesn't grow on trees, you know." Later, when the Second World War started, Douglas referred to his request and added that "when money was needed to prosecute a war, the government soon found the trees on which money grew."

Dust and windstorms ravaged the west, sweeping all the fertile topsoil from farm after farm. It left what was termed a "dust bowl" and the scourge of rust invaded the wheat crops. I have witnessed the latter on a large farm near eastern Saskatchewan, where the owner took me dejectedly to a small knoll in the middle of acres and acres of wheat, completely ruined. In the extreme west, hundreds of transients had remained in Vancouver and Victoria where the climate provided a sanctuary from the bitter prairie winter.

There seemed to be not one glimmer of hope in the desolation of the economy and widespread malaise pervaded the whole nation. Perhaps it was this depressing undercurrent, which set men talking of communism, or a violent uprising which nurtured radical social trends in Parliament, giving birth to increased pensions for the aged and disabled, incomes for the unemployed, Medicare and greater Welfare Benefits. There is no doubt that many of these were stop-gap measures, but I feel confident that a more comprehensive plan will one day be put into operation to save administrative costs.

Many unfortunate incidents resulted during the hungry thirties out of sheer desperation. One of these was the killing of Evans in Regina during the "On to Ottawa" march. I was in Winnipeg during that time and I witnessed an orderly, but heart-rending parade by these frustrated citizens. They walked along Portage Avenue and through the Hudson Bay Store, with a dark hopelessness on all of their faces.

The winter, dreadfully morbid and long, as only city winters can be, dragged through its weary course. Christmas, even in the absence of a benevolent Santa Claus, seemed to give a glimmer of joy and hope in the faces of people to whom their memory of happier "Noels" was remembered. My sister bought a small tree and decided to wait until the last few minutes of Christmas Eve before purchasing a turkey. Bargain prices would then, no doubt, be offered in the stores, especially on perishables.

Promptly, at four-thirty, we embarked on a search for our Christmas turkey, chicken, goose or whatever. In the second store we entered, we saw an almost unbelievable sight - a large, fat goose, weighing eight pounds, five ounces, had been reduced from six dollars and fifty cents to two dollars and fifty cents because of a missing leg. Naturally, we purchased it and carried it home quite proudly.

The presents on Christmas Day were few, a handkerchief for Sis with small flowers woven in the corner and a pocketknife for me. Stewart, her husband, received a pouch of tobacco, and the goose with trimmings needless to say provided ample fare. We enjoyed a Yuletide meal I shall long remember.

In February of 1935, I discovered that Mr. Ralph Parsons, the Chief Factor with the Hudson Bay Fur Trade, (with offices and warehouse located in Winnipeg), would be in Toronto for a couple of days, so I decided to contact him for possible employment. He was related to me, so I thought this might lend added weight to my appeal. He proved very sympathetic and phoned the next day to say that he would give me a job in the Winnipeg warehouse, though for how long, he did not know. The wage was to be eighteen cents an hour for a ten-hour day. He issued a railway ticket and in two days, I was on my way west again, although this time under entirely different circumstances.

Arriving in Winnipeg, with the temperature hovering around thirty-five degrees below zero Fahrenheit, I secured a room in the Fort Gary Apartments, about two city blocks from the Fur Trade Building on Main Street. Mr. William Scorer, a veteran of the Riel Rebellion, his wife and son, Stuart, occupied the remainder of the apartment. They were very kind people, doing everything possible to make me feel at home. The old lady died of old age in April, and Mr. Scorer and Stuart moved to Selkirk, where they had close relatives. Mr. Scorer gave me two infantry swords used in the Rebellion. These disappeared later in one of my many moves in Toronto.

Moving to a room on Vaughan Street, I stayed there for the remainder of service with the Hudson Bay Company. My work consisted mainly of crating goods that were to be sent to the various trading posts strung along the territory from Hudson Bay to the Rockies. The names Lac la Rouge, Rupert House, Sioux Lookout and Il a La Crosse are names that will live forever in my memory.

In June of 1935, one of the saddest events of my life occurred. My benefactress, Miss Christine Fellows, died of cancer in Bradwell, England. We had corresponded regularly, and had I been able, would have gone to see her. She left me a few shares in the Hudson Bay Company, which, would soon prove to be most useful in starting me on my way of becoming a veterinarian. In September, six of us who had been most recently employed, were told that due to the economic situation, we would no longer be needed.

Taking my small savings of shares and armed with my Chadacre Agricultural Certificate, I headed for the Ontario Veterinary College at Guelph, Ontario, about sixty miles from Toronto.

*Nathan Budgell, DVM*

# CHAPTER X - UNIVERSITY

Dr. C. A. MacGilvray was then President of Guelph University and I approached him directly, stating how anxious I was to enroll, and that my past experience and training in farming should be quite an asset. Although the full complement of new students had already been met, he entered me at once in the freshman class of 1935.

Being adept at soccer, I joined the Ontario Agricultural College, Soccer Eleven, as a right half. This proved to be my greatest asset in extra-curricular activities. Finances were very strained and after paying my fees of 250 dollars, buying books and supplies I had very little money left. I managed, however, to find a part-time job looking after two horses for a lady who worked for the Guelph Mercury Company - the pay two dollars a week. I would feed and water the horses, morning, noon and night, Monday through Friday, and groom and exercise them on Saturday. She would often ride them on weekends and generally look after them on Sundays. This small income looked after my room rent.

After each soccer practice, and following lectures, I would retire to the student dining room at the Agricultural College, moving with the student throng (unnoticed by the Dean), and there take excellent meals. Leftovers were meticulously stuffed around my being, taken to my room, and later heated up on my kitchen hot plate. Almost every Saturday we visited neighbouring universities like McMaster, Western and Toronto for inter-university games. On these occasions, I arranged to have the horses looked after.

When winter really set in during late October, I reflected how my soccer record had enabled me, through having to practice and spend time in the College gym, to escape the rather childish initiation of the freshmen by students of the sophomore year. One practice was to have to propel peanuts, by nose pushing, along the main street in Guelph, resulting often in temporary disfigurement and physical pain to one's nose.

Another means of initiation was to hold the freshman upside down, with his head in the "bog" toilet and flush it while several idiots chanted some incantation about being welcomed into the learned company of intelligentsia attending the University. Frosh caps and placards had to be worn, at all times, for a period of six weeks. These, and several other initiation "musts," were endured by the frosh for fear of actual physical cruelty if not tolerated. The following year, I was asked to serve on the Initiation Committee, but refused to do so with the excuses of soccer practice, boxing, gymnastics and cross-country running. Actually, I abhorred the ritual and have never convinced myself, over the years, that it served any useful purpose.

My extra-curricular activities during the first and second winters consisted of boxing and soccer at the indoor stadium in town. These, of course, gave me access to the dining room for the greater part of each week. Many friends there also contributed to my welfare by concealing buns and the like for me to take home later. In the interim, I ate plenty of vegetable beef soup, costing five cents a tin.

Potatoes and turnips were gleaned from a neighbouring farmer's field, during the early autumn moonlight hours. My room mate or I would keep watch, while the other in turn would crawl along the vegetable rows, pulling a sack, which we would partly fill. Occasionally a sudden loud barking in our vicinity would cause us to make a hurried exit. Before the really cold weather set in, we had obtained a plentiful supply of produce, which lasted us most of the winter.

The Ontario Agriculture College was conducting fattening ration tests on hundreds of poultry, the "Plymouth Rock" variety, so a few of these too found their way into our delicious stews. Steaks were a rarity, but occasionally we allowed ourselves the luxury of one at twelve cents a pound. My classmate, Norman Scollard, and I were invited out, once weekly, to play bridge with two dear old ladies living near the college. Although we enjoyed playing the game, the royal feast of sandwiches and cake always followed, leaving an indelible mark in my memory. I concluded, in later years, that they were fully aware of our dire straits, as our attempt at being good bridge players, was glaringly apparent. Hoyle would have dubbed us pure masqueraders.

I thoroughly enjoyed studies and did not find the first and second years too difficult as they were mainly centered around animal husbandry. I had already studied these quite extensively at Chadacre in England. The third and fourth years were more difficult, but intensely interesting as they involved practical application of theory.

At the end of the first year, I realized that I simply had to find employment for the summer. I could at least count on food if I was accepted once again in the Soccer Eleven, but there were books to be purchased and my room expenses would have to be met. I made several fruitless attempts to find work, until one day, a large printed ad in the Toronto Star caught my eye. It told of phenomenal profits to be realized by selling a deodorizer and disinfectant called "De-Odour X" to owners and inhabitants of summer cottages. Weary city dwellers did not want to endure the discomfort of odours from smelly latrines or toilets in fairly close proximity to their dwellings. Convince them that the "De-Odour X" would overcome this nuisance, and a sale was almost certain, with a return of seventy-five cents from a bottle costing two dollars and fifty cents. The only conditions were that the salesman must be bonded and possess a car. At that time I was chumming with a friend called George Joel, who lived in west Toronto, and thought we could do a good job of selling.

*Nathan Budgell, DVM*

His father offered him a 1933 Pontiac Sedan; we were on our way! We went to see Fred Bannerman on Dundas Street, told him of our desire to work hard, convinced him of our honesty, and loaded the car. We had two-hundred pint sprinkle bottles, a tent and a few cans of food. With these, we headed for Wasaga Beach and other points.

The hot June weather that we hoped would be followed by an even hotter July and August, would provide a perfect environment for our sales pitch and ultimate sales. George was rather shy and pleaded with me to approach the first object of persuasion, an elderly lady, very prim and proper. We could plainly see the one-holer a short distance behind the trim little cottage. After telling her what a most wonderful product I was selling, she just stood there giving me a dubious look, so I finally convinced her to accompany me to the "out house" for a demonstration. I would sprinkle the "De-Odour X" in the hole, then after five minutes we would again give it the smell test, sort of the before and after test, or now you smell it and now you don't - it worked! The first two bottles were deposited hurriedly on her kitchen counter, while a five-dollar bill burnt itself into the palm of my hand. It is said that nothing succeeds like success and before the day ended, the super sales staff of Budgell and Joel, had sold thirty-five bottles and covered eighty cottages. Some clients could detect no change, and for that matter, to be quite frank, neither could we.

We made a hurried exit from Wasaga Beach that night, in case some of our customers decided it was not such a good investment after all, and maybe spot us among the crowd of vacationers. We camped, covering the rest of the area the next day, then on to Barrie and Lake Simcoe. Sales resistance seemed to increase when we hit Barrie and a great calamity befell us there. Transmission trouble developed, forcing us to run in second gear. The car would not reverse and repairs, we were told, would amount to forty-eight stupendous dollars. To date, we had disposed of 120 bottles of the ninety dollars profit, we had spent half for food, gas and oil.

When the repairs were made, we gave the garage twenty-five dollars and fifteen bottles of our mixture for the balance. Enough gas to fill the tank was then purchased at fifteen cents a gallon and we were again on our way. It took three days to cover cottages around Lake Simcoe and when we ended up back in Toronto, we had thirty dollars between us to show for our days on the road. As well, we were now thoroughly convinced that selling was not our forte. Bannerman was the smartest as his cost was twenty cents per bottle. He had earned through our efforts, a total of 410 dollars. We decided to look for something a bit more profitable.

George obtained work, a permanent job, as a stock clerk in the downtown warehouse. I read an ad asking for a wood finisher. It required one to remove old stains, varnish and paint down to the natural surface, then resurface it again. This was in an older house on St. Clair Avenue. I phoned and was asked to come over for an interview. I was admitted into the impressive old mansion standing back from the street and surmised that it had once been the residence of people of good means. Two concrete flower urns stood at the gates and a circular drive led to the front door. A rather elderly lady, and her partly paralyzed husband, welcomed me into the drawing room, a room filled with substantial furniture looking the worse for wear. A large balustrade guarded a spacious stairway leading to the upper portion of the house. Everywhere there was mahogany and basswood, which evidently had been painted and varnished several times. Spots of chipping were evident everywhere, but I was confident that with lots of paint remover and elbow grease, I could manage to scrape and sand it off. The couple was willing to pay me 150 dollars and I figured it would take me about ten days. I provided myself with the necessary material and began my arduous chore.

It took four days just to do one doorframe and there were eight such demons with which to wrestle. On the sixth day, my arms felt devoid of all muscle, my hands were badly callused and the smell of paint remover had penetrated to the very depth of my lungs. I quit! - pure and simple and did not return on the seventh day. Like the good Lord, I had worked hard performing a super-human task for six days and decided I needed a rest on the seventh. I wonder, to this day, whether the dear old couple persuaded someone else to finish the work. Even the pay ceased to be important for that feat.

My next job was on a farm in Markham, near Toronto, where I worked for six weeks, fourteen to sixteen hours daily for twenty cents an hour. No pay was forthcoming, however, until after the ten-hour period. Working for two dollars a day and meals, seven days a week, I managed to save some seventy-five dollars to begin my second year at university.

On September 4, I left the farm and called in on my sister who washed and ironed my clothes sending me hitch-hiking back to Guelph. I traveled lightly as I owned barely enough clothes to cover my back. This year passed much the same as the first, eating because of soccer and tending the same horses.

From time to time, during the winter, I hitchhiked into Toronto to see my sister. One of these times, a couple offered me a ride back to Guelph. The only room they had for me was in the trunk of their car. Getting in, I managed to wedge myself securely and sixty miles further was let out. Being January, I was practically paralyzed with the cold and I literally fell out of the trunk. Painfully making my way home I walked on the sides of my feet as the soles were totally without feeling, absolutely numb.

Part of my second summer was spent with a preceptor, Dr. H. Culp, who had a small veterinary practice. He was rather elderly and he paid me thirty dollars per week to act as the kennel man and general assistant. A month later, a Dr. A.J. Campbell, another veterinarian, invited me to work for him in his clinic on Gerrard Street in Toronto. I was to be a live-in student and was to receive forty dollars per week, plus a room over the clinic. I thought this a generous stipend as

I was quite aware that he was in financial difficulties. The drug houses requested a deposit or straight cash for orders. Dr. Campbell would ask me to peer cautiously through the doorway into the waiting room to be sure there was not a salesman calling for a deposit on an outstanding account. If there was such a one, I was to inform him that the doctor was in surgery, or out on an emergency. I think that most of the salesmen knew the score and often laughed, or remarked loudly enough, for old Campbell to hear, "I'll call on him again, thank you."

My financial circumstances were considerably better on entering my third year at the university. I found little time for off-campus activities. In the spring of 1938, I thought it might be a good idea to go to England for the purpose of renewing old acquaintances.

A good friend of mine in charge of the Department of Transport, in Quebec City, a Mr. Jacob Kane, helped me find a way. He was very interested in dog sled racing and had developed a fast runner at crossing Huskies with Great Danes. They had speed, but did not inherit the tough feet of the Husky. I had given him good advice on how to overcome foot wounds by using one of my preparations. He informed me that an old icebreaker, the Mikula, was leaving for Scotland early in May and was to be broken up for scrap. He got me a job as assistant steward, which even paid me fifty dollars for the trip.

How the ship passed as seaworthy I will never know. The lifeboats were ancient and daylight could be seen through seams on their sides. No wireless was available in case of emergency, there were no stabilizers, so the hull wallowed in the ocean like a whale sometimes rolling so far that the sea would wash over the deck. Only the bare necessities were left to provide a modicum of comfort for the motley crew. The latter had been garnered from the streets of Quebec and Montreal, many being utterly ignorant regarding the art of seamanship.

# CHAPTER XI - ENGLAND AGAIN

We left Quebec City on April 24 and headed for Sydney Mines, Nova Scotia, in order to take on coal. Captain Reith, a retired veteran of service on the Lady Line of Ships in the Caribbean tourist service, commanded the ship. Two days off Cape Race, Newfoundland, we ran into a terrific storm. I was convinced that the old tub would roll over completely. Many of the crew, unfamiliar with the sea, were violently ill. It was most difficult to navigate the stairs leading to the bridge while balancing a tray laden with tea and sandwiches for the officers on the bridge. My bunk was athwart the ship so that, at times, I would be standing on my head or my feet in the bunk. The miraculous thing is that I was never seasick and ate up to six huge meals daily.

A rumor circulated, after about ten days that the crewmembers were in a mutinous state due to the deplorable living conditions in their quarters - rats were running rampant. I had been told that no bedding, other than a thin mattress, had been provided. The owner of the Mikula had been counting on a fast crossing of about six days.

The ship was capable of seventeen knots, but adverse weather slowed progress for two days to three knots in the teeth of a vicious northeast gale. Always in mind, was the fear that we could disappear, without a trace, with no means of contacting any sources of help. On the seventeenth day after steaming through schools of hungry-looking sharks, we spotted at dusk the light on Malin Head, Northern Ireland. Entering the calm waters of the North Channel and moving up into the Firth of Clyde we tied up at a pier near Glasgow. Many people lining the banks thought we were a gunboat returning from service with the Loyalist Forces in the Spanish Civil War. The armour-plated Mikula, with its grey paint could convey such an impression.

I saw the Queen Mary at that time being built at Greenoch, in John Brown's Ship Yard. Immediately on docking, a wrecking squad started dismantling our ancient vessel. Its structure to be used in forging weapons of war, the clouds of which loomed on the horizon. I took the train to Edinburgh and spent the four hours waiting for a connection to Great Yarmouth, visiting the famous castle, park and the statue of Sir Walter Scott. I found the capital city most beautiful, vivid with the colour of tulips and daffodils contrasting with the brilliant greens of late spring.

My trip to Great Yarmouth, through the lovely Lake District, Yorkshire Moors, Fenlands of Lincolnshire, and finally the rich agricultural lands of Norfolk and Suffolk, is one I shall long remember.

Arriving in the city, I went to the home of Mr. Henry Fellows, owner of the dry-docks. My delight in seeing everybody again overwhelmed me. Mrs. Castell, niece of Miss Fellows, living in a rambling old house across the road from Mr.

Henry, had asked me to stay with her. Her husband, Rex, a science professor at Taunton University died very suddenly, leaving her with three small children: John, David and Margaret, or "Dee," as she was fondly called. Mr. Henry gave me part-time work in the yard office, leaving me plenty of time to visit many of the dear people I had known during my school days in Bradwell.

On two occasions I went to London, visiting Miss Spalding at the offices of the Grenfell Association, 82 Victoria Street. While there I once again viewed the famous old landmarks such as Westminster Abbey, St. Paul's Cathedral, Buckingham Palace and Canada House. Returning to Great Yarmouth I spent as much time as possible with the Castell children, whom I felt missed their father a great deal. One afternoon, I cycled out to Somerleyton Hall. Many of the gardeners were still busily employed, but I was saddened to hear that Lord Somerleyton had died. I met her Ladyship walking through the park near the private chapel and she was delighted to see me, asking me to tea during which she expressed great interest in my travels.

The Castell children enjoyed immensely our jaunts through the countryside. We would follow the embankment or "Dyke" built to keep back the waters of the River Yare, down to the ruins of Burgh Castle, where we would search for Roman coins and pottery in the fields. The river always had its quota of wherries or barges, taking mustard to Norwich for processing. Their unhurried pace by sail, filled one with a sense of tranquillity and contentment. The children would enjoy Stone Ginger Beer and sandwiches on these expeditions, which, were complete studies in nature. Animals and birds of many varieties abounded and I was bombarded with puzzling questions as to their ultimate winter destinations, if any.

The God of War in the form of German military resurgence was beginning to plant its feet on the sacred soil of many states of the European continent. Areas formerly occupied by Germany were being annexed to the Fatherland, under the leadership of Adolf Hitler. The swastika became to those, not of German blood, a symbol of fear and tyranny. Jews were blamed for all of the ills besetting Germany, and were singled out for unheard of persecution, and ultimate extermination. Neville Chamberlain returned from Munich with his compromise "Peace in our time" agreement, but the whole continent seemed to be edging, ever closer, to the brink of war. England, in my view, abhorred the thought of another conflict, perhaps more terrible than the First World War, some twenty years earlier.

The government began an active recruiting campaign sending detachments of army personnel and equipment on a tour of the British Isles, hoping to arouse the populace to the fact that trouble was imminent. The response was lethargic as the people simply did not want to become involved. Hitler, however, continued his relentless march towards his ultimate doom. It is said that the British Lion can stand a lot of tail twisting, but if twisted once too often, woe betides the twister.

Such was the outcome about a year later when the people of England, aghast at happenings in Nazi Germany, decided to go to the aid of humans being maliciously, and without reason, slaughtered or subjugated by what Churchill described as "that evil man."

August came and it was time to return to Canada and my final year in university. I had grown very fond of the Castell children. Rex and I had been very close, both being fond of long-distance running, which we shared together on many occasions. John went on to become a psychiatrist, David a psychologist and "Dee," after graduating in economics from the University of London, married and settled down, quite happily, in Caistore near Great Yarmouth.

Through friends of the Constantine Line, I managed to secure a berth on the S.S. Hazelwood, a cargo ship of eight thousand tons, carrying a load of anthracite coal from Swansea in Wales, to Quebec City. The trip of twelve days, was fairly uneventful, except for running into a howling gale in the Devil's Cauldron area, about five hundred miles southwest of Ireland. It is said to be one of the deepest and most turbulent spots in the Atlantic. At times, I thought the sturdy vessel would never lift its bow above the weight of water into which it would plunge. Hour after hour heading into the teeth of the gale, we made barely one knot an hour for twenty-seven hours. Day after long day tossing, plunging and sloping sideways, into deep watery troughs, we finally entered the calm waters of the Gulf of St. Lawrence.

Quebec City, with its quaint waterfront and commanding bastion on the Plains of Abraham, was a welcome sight filling one with a sense of thankfulness in being privileged to be a citizen of this great country. Canada can truly be called "Heaven Blessed," a land of opportunity for people of all races and creeds.

## CHAPTER XII - AFTER GRADUATION

My final year at the university was quite uneventful and passed all too quickly. I had become a member of a worthy profession and always having been an individualist, decided to strike out on my own rather than seek the security of a government job. Jobs in the Health of Animals Branch of the Federal Civil Service were at that time being offered for sixteen hundred dollars a year. I recollect one of the professors at the O.A.C. admonishing us that we were graduating with the power to "sink, burn or destroy," whatever that meant, but to do it wisely. I little realized, until some years later, the implication of those words. Professionals, especially those dealing with life and death, have the power to direct markedly the emotional course of whole families or individuals in time of loss, and there were times when my colleagues and I resorted to little white lies, to avoid a complete emotional or physical breakdown.

On hearing that a small practice set up in a garage at the rear of the Bailey residence, on Mount Pleasant and Eglinton Avenues in Toronto was for sale, I inquired as to the terms. Dr. Bailey had died a year previously and his daughter, Jacqueline, continued to use the building for grooming dogs. I was more interested in acquiring instruments and winning back the clientele, so I made an offer of one thousand dollars, plus a lease for five years.

I found the quarters inadequate, especially in winter. The heating consisted of a small coke burning stove which often had to be stoked three or four times at night during the cold weather. During these periods, I would put up a small cot in the operating room and respond to the alarm of a sudden decline in the temperature, which caused me to wake up frequently. Fortunately for me, the Baileys decided to put their house up for sale, and told me, in case of a concrete offer, they would not hold me to the lease.

This happened in April of 1940 and I then approached a Dr. Fred Bridgeman who operated a practice in Toronto at the corner of Manor Road and Yonge Street. I wanted the possibility of entering into a partnership with him. He seemed quite taken with the idea, as it would enable both of us to take time off occasionally. The practice was called the North Toronto Veterinary Hospital. It was here that I found there were many more factors than merely treating an animal that had to be considered in our profession.

Owners were so emotionally attached to their pets that the loss of one could well have tragic effects. One owner remarked when I asked him why he spent all his time with his sporting dogs, rather than cultivate closer relations with his neighbours said, "I tried people." It reminded me about the well-known poem about a dog that went like this:

"No better friend I'll ever find,
Nor one that's half so good and kind
Than my old dog that day by day,
Grows fonder of me every way."

On occasion certain things which by the rules of the book, were said to be very unprofessional, had to be employed for humane reasons. One incident involved a small poodle whose owner had died, and whose husband, a sergeant in the army, was away quite often. The dog was her constant companion and on her deathbed the good lady asked that the dog's ashes also be interred on top of her grave upon its death. About six months later, the poor little creature died seemingly through sheer loneliness as no symptoms of illness were apparent. It had been boarding with me as the husband had moved out west leaving a forwarding address and telephone number in case of an emergency. I tried to trace him for a week while keeping the dog in the refrigerator but all was in vain. After nine days, I disposed of the body and the day after, who should phone but the sergeant hearing about the demise, informing me of her last wish.

I have known tough sergeants in the army who would never under any circumstances shed a tear, but here was an exception. He broke down completely and asked if I still had the body. I spontaneously said "yes," and set in motion a little white lie, which I found difficult to extricate myself. He asked if I would cremate the dog and put the ashes in a jar, thereby carrying out her wish. I assured him it would be done, and visited a butcher friend of mine who suggested I take a couple of cow hocks, reduce them to ashes in the coal furnace used for heating at that time, and bury them as requested. Neighbours must have been mystified by the noxious smell of smoke emanating from my chimney on a hot August day.

I had attended the lady's funeral and subsequent interment, so found no difficulty in sequestering the precious package about my person, visiting the cemetery just at dusk, when others were leaving. I hurriedly dug a hole with a small trowel and deposited the jar several inches deep, carefully replacing the sod. Two weeks later on his return, the sergeant could not thank me enough, and on returning from the grave site, called on me, whereupon we adjourned to a local pub where he compensated me well, with both cash and beer.

I remember some quite harrowing experiences during the early days of practice. Once when I was conducting operations at the first establishment in the Bailey garage, a large German Shepherd was brought in. He had bitten several people and the police decided to have him destroyed. Constantine, a kennel man working for me then, who had no greater qualifications than the gift of the gab, admitted the animal and dragged him into the back kennel room where I happened to be. The room had a cage capacity of twelve, including two large ones, which were vacant at the time. At the doorway of the room, the dog suddenly turned his head, bared his fangs, and attacked my helper. This proved too much for the gentleman, and he propelled the beast, with the help of his boot, into the kennel room and hurriedly shut the door.

For a moment the dog and I stared at each other, neither of us moving. I spoke to him and opened the cage door that he approached until he realized that it was for him. Low growls and sharp fangs cautioned me to move back to the other end of the room, which I did very quietly. I shouted to the kennel man to assist me, but he concluded that discretion was the better part of valor, and refused to come to my aid. A small pot belly coke burning stove was located by the door to the outside exit of the room, and on a shelf, immediately above, was a little hatchet which I used to split kindling. The dog by this time was letting me know in mean fashion, that he intended to find a way out of his confined space. Other inmates of the cages did nothing to help, by their constant yelping. I grabbed the axe just as the animal made a leap for the door, intending to make short work of anything in its path. I could not move aside and I felt his sharp fangs tear at my long white coat, by my shoulder. With my knee, I temporarily winded him, knocking him to the floor. He recovered quickly and once more lunged at me, but this time I was prepared. I hit him with the axe on the head, stunning him, and quickly tied a gag around his mouth, instructing the kennel man, who by this time thought I had parted this world, or at least, been severely bitten, to bring a syringe of lethal solution, which instantly dispatched him.

One other incident that stands out very clearly in my mind, occurred when I was in practice in Toronto. A very good client who owned a poodle, worked as a secretary downtown. She lived not far from my clinic and as companion to a stockbroker who was very fond of the bottle. One afternoon she phoned to say her pet had been feeling under the weather, and would I do her a favour by going to her house, and pick up the dog. She would collect it later when she came from work. She added that the gentleman should be home, but was probably sleeping off a bout with the bottle.

Knocking at the front and side door brought no response. I concluded the dog that was quite old was either very ill or possibly dead. After scouting around, I noticed an open basement window. It was easy access, so I entered, landing on a heap of coal, used to fuel the furnace. Concluding that the owner was out, I walked gingerly toward the stairs leading to what I presumed was the kitchen area. It was quite dark at that end of the basement and I must have made enough noise to awaken the owner from his reverie. The lady had warned me that he sometimes kept a revolver at hand for fear of intruders. I heard the tramp of heavy feet toward the cellar and the light switched on in the basement. He demanded to know who was there and that he would shoot first and look after. I ran as fast as possible back to the window and frantically tried to get out, hampered by the fact that the coal kept giving way as I tried to climb to the window. However, I managed to spring out, almost flying, just as I heard the footsteps on the coal behind me - a close call.

Dr. Bridgeman retired from the practice in 1942, due to ill health. Even copious doses of Betavin, a concentrated elixir of vitamins and minerals in a port wine base, which we purchased in gallon quantities for kennel use, could not restore him to vibrant health. I purchased his share of the practice and after eighteen months entered the Royal Canadian Army Medical Corps. I engaged one Dr. Harold Gibbs, to conduct my practice until my return one year later.

England was standing with her back to the wall and Churchill had vowed she would fight, with every conceivable weapon and position, until the evil of Nazism was destroyed. I enlisted on a wave of emotionalism then sweeping Canada, fed by the singing of such songs as "There'll always be an England" and "The White Cliffs of Dover." The tough little island was indeed fighting the battle of its life, trying to stem the Nazis, in their bid to subjugate all of Europe, including England, and then the world. France had given up the fight, leaving airfields and seaports for enemy use. Nothing it seemed stood between a German victory except the indomitable will of the British people and the loyalty of the Commonwealth.

This two-year period of my army life, included rigorous basic training and trying to run a practice of Veterinary Science in the evenings with my assistant. I was discharged in 1945 due to a gastric ulcer and resumed my practice full-time. Dr. Gibbs, my assistant, left for Hamilton, Ontario where he became engaged in a successful practice lasting many years.

## CHAPTER XIII - COURTSHIP

In April of 1945 an event occurred which was to change my pattern of life. I became attracted to a young lady named Florence Hull, daughter of a dentist, Richard Hull, engaged in a practice on the corner of Yonge and Bloor Streets. He was a very possessive father but married to a beautiful and understanding wife. Florence was called Sharrie for most of her life because she had been named after a step-grandmother that tried to rifle their grandfather's estate. The family decided to call her Sharrie instead and this has stayed with us throughout.

Sharrie's grandfather, a Grand Master of the Masonic Lodge, had accumulated a considerable fortune in the shoe sales, repair and real estate business, a man of integrity and well respected. Her father was quite authoritative making no question of the fact that he was head of the house and all those dwelling therein. Churchillian in manner and looks, even to the point of smoking sixteen cigars a day, he would stroll down the street wearing his camel hair coat, hamburg hat, cane, and invariably a Daschund on a leash at his side. One day during World War II when on his daily constitution with his dog, he overtook two elderly ladies who obviously disliked everything German. One was heard to remark that the poor creature was German, "look at that man with a German dog." Dick Hull turned and advised them that it was indeed German, and also the "captain of a submarine."

Dr. Hull's three lovely daughters led sheltered lives, and Dick would have been quite satisfied to have them at home on a permanent basis. His birthday was on Dominion Day, July 1. On this day a large sign was prominently displayed on the veranda reading "Peace on earth, goodwill to men, Dick Hull's birthday's here again," inviting all passersby in for a drink. He rarely allowed his daughters out after dark, a fact which brought down his wrath on both Sharrie and me when we decided to watch the lights go out in Toronto during one of the early blackouts. Her brother squealed on us and she was confined to barracks for a whole week.

Another time when she was ill in bed with a bad cold, I thought it would be nice to see her. I knocked on the door and hearing no welcoming voice, stepped inside and proceeded to ascend the stairs. A stentorian voice cautioned "Do not do that!" and I turned to find him standing in the middle of the living room. I pointedly told him that I had every right to do so and would proceed to her room. This I did and awhile afterwards he told Sharrie that I was a determined son of a gun, but admired my courage. At other times, when he accosted me on the street, he advised me not to see Sharrie again, but like a ship in the teeth of a howling gale I persisted, even when he threatened to break every bone in my body and tear me limb from limb.

Our courtship could have been made a best-selling novel as many amusing things happened during the three years we sort of courted when no one knew but Sharrie's mother. One time Sharrie and I decided to go away for a weekend with her mother joining us. She had convinced her father that her girlfriends Babe, Willy and she would bolster the war effort by picking peaches during the summer. Dick allowed her to go and I had no problem picking her up at the farm where she worked. Dick however, smelled a rat, so he put her mother on the train thinking she was going to visit her sister up in Georgian Bay.

Mother got on the train at Union Station and got off in New Toronto where Sharrie and I were waiting in the car. Away we happily went for the weekend, and no one was any the wiser. There were many other times like this.

**Figure 16 Florence (Sharrie) Hull, myself (Nathan) with my future in-laws Elizabeth (Jennings) Hull and Dr. Richard Hull.**

On another occasion I visited the family, Sharrie and her mother, sitting in the kitchen, heard the front door knob rattle. Without a sound, I jumped up, raced out the back door, and leaped the fence, walking to my practice only a block away. It is said that "all's well that ends well." Sharrie and I were married on April 7, 1945, in Glebe Road United Church. Persisting to the very end, Dick Hull cautioned Sharrie in the vestibule of the church, and all the way down the aisle, "It's not too late to change your mind," thereby delaying the service for ten long minutes as I stood at the front of the aisle.

Our honeymoon was spent in New York City, and we enjoyed visiting many of its famous landmarks. Celebration was somewhat dampened, however, owing to the death of President Franklin D. Roosevelt. This we heard quite by accident as we were in an elevator. The heart of the great metropolis literally stopped beating, as did that of the whole nation. No deeper sorrow could have been felt by those millions of Americans who had come to love and respect this great man.

**Figure 17 My future wife, Florence Hull.**

My wife Sharrie had wanted to pursue Veterinary Science as a vocation. Because the college at that time was totally made up of male students, her father soon put the kibosh on that idea. After a period of three years, before we started a family, Sharrie had acquired a good knowledge of the practical side of the sciences while working by my side as receptionist and surgical assistant.

It was then that I decided to take a two-week vacation in Newfoundland. I hired a recent graduate of the Veterinary College who, with Sharrie, would care for my practice during my absence. A memorable trip to say the least, visiting all the old sites by train and steamer rather than on foot as I had done a few years earlier.

During my absence a cat, heavy with kittens, having great difficulty in delivering, was admitted. It was obvious that a Caesarian section was demanded. The newly graduated veterinarian, surgical book at hand, plus Sharrie's experience with the practical side performed a perfect operation delivering four thriving kittens.

The years following our marriage brought about a deep understanding between Dick Hull and myself. I always had a sneaking regard for him, and grew to admire his finer qualities. We went on many fishing trips, one of which severely tested his sense of humour.

We were on a chartered boat at Meaford in Georgian Bay fishing for lake trout. A long copper line with a spoon attached at the end trailed behind the slow moving craft, and in turn was tied to a bell on the side of the cabin. When a fish was hooked the bell would ring and the process of winding in two hundred feet of line on a large wheel would begin. Dick had decided to answer the call of nature, and entered the small cubicle near the cabin. I concluded he was well settled, as was his wont, and gave a vigorous tug on the line. The loud ringing denoted a fish of prize proportions. A loud roar sounded from the inner sanctum, followed by a very excited apparition emerging from the doorway, puffing, and holding on to his trousers as well as an enormous cigar. It was impossible to hide our amusement, and a torrent of phrases in no uncertain terms, cautioned us that we had carried the practical joke a little too far, at a most inopportune time. However, he retracted when shortly after we caught eleven beautiful trout, each weighing no less than nine pounds.

Returning to Toronto, I resumed practice at my new location in Willowdale, about six miles out of the city. I built an animal hospital there, and enjoyed a healthy practice. The years there were quite uneventful, but there were building problems prior to starting practice. Strikes on the part of plumbers, builders and electricians delayed completion to a point where it seemed that nothing could go right. Pranksters on Halloween pushed down a newly erected wall, plumbers quit when the heating system was sorely needed to finish the inside work, and heaving frost moved an outside stairway half an inch over onto a neighbour's property, delaying the last mortgage draw.

When I finally moved in after four months of frustrating delays, I couldn't have cared less if a bomb had leveled the whole structure. These, and other experiences since, have convinced me that unions, of whatever nature, should be severely restricted and subject to arbitration. Work stoppage should certainly not be allowed, as it hits the little fellow who can ill afford to be a pawn in their so-called justifiable bellyaching.

To accentuate this attitude, I well remember an occasion when I was operating a large farm in Newfoundland having some twenty thousand laying hens. I had ordered a carload of feed from Nova Scotia which because of bad weather, or act of God, whichever, had not arrived on time. Unfortunately it did arrive on the morning of a countrywide Canadian National Railways strike. I had very little feed left, and being fully aware of the cannibalistic habit of hens deprived of food, envisaged the loss of a good part of my flock. Pickets were set up at the yards in Cornerbrook. I did everything possible to persuade the union and management to let me take enough feed out of my carload to tide me over for the weekend, they refused point-blank. Local situations did not enter into the picture. I finally gleaned whatever feed I could from other producers who were also running short. By the time the strike ended on Monday afternoon, I had lost two thousand through crowding and cannibalism.

I always wanted to return to Newfoundland, and after attending the Confederation banquet on the eve of the union with Canada, at the Royal York Hotel, March 31, 1949, the urge became even greater. Many prominent politicians spoke of the many advantages to be gained from the union, and no doubt there were many, but they emphasized that it meant the addition and welcoming of almost 500,000 citizens of Anglo-Saxon stock to the population of Canada. The stroke of twelve midnight would usher in a new dawn for the former Dominion of Newfoundland, lovingly called the "Old Rock" by its citizens, a hardy God-fearing people.

After almost five hundred years of wresting a living from the cruel sea, the tragic consequences which are recorded in the annals of history. Brave men facing death daily on the ice floes in search of seals, or that of ships disappearing without a trace while fishing, bringing sadness and loss to whole communities season after season. As the years followed over the centuries, a heritage worthy of daring men was woven into the fabric of a proud people. Their ships ventured into the seaports of faraway lands, taking on cargoes of precious salt fish to the numerous markets of Europe, or to the islands in the Caribbean. This way of life was at times meager, but the hope always remained that catches and prices would be better the next year, spurring them on at length. Their patriotic devotion to the Motherland was never wanting, her sons responded always to the call of duty whenever needed. Their sacrifices on the battlefields of Europe and in great naval engagements, were without parallel. July 1 commemorates the battle of Beaumont Hamel in the First World War, where almost seven hundred of a regiment of eight hundred lost their lives. That day is known as "Memorial Day" and is the day when proud citizens pay homage to their memory.

Hardship encountered every day seemed to knit these simple people of this small island into a close family unit. I sensed this feeling in the breasts of all those assembled in the ballroom of the Royal York on that landmark evening. There was hardly a dry eye when the "Ode to Newfoundland" was sung for the last time as the national anthem, and the strains of "O Canada" told all present that a great era had ended. Very few knew the words or tune of the Canadian anthem, but true patriot love was quickly exemplified on the part of Canada's newest province, and Britain's oldest colony.

Today old timers still talk of going up to Canada when leaving the island. Many benefits ensued from Confederation. Development of the vast forest and mineral wealth was accelerated, and the spectra of want and privation encompassing old age, prolonged illness and unemployment was removed. Education facilities were vastly improved and universities and trade schools were established. Premier Joseph R. Smallwood, a man of great vision, knew full well the dream of a fuller life, which would result from union with the great Canadian federation. Subsequent years have proved that his dream was not without substance.

I have considered it an honour and privilege to have known this last great father of confederation for a number of years. He will likely be remembered as the greatest Newfoundland premier of all time. Others succeeding him may attain fame through the discovery and development of rich assets such as minerals, oil and gas but largely through funds provided by a paternal Federal government. Joey Smallwood had to start from scratch with a vision of an enlightened people free of poverty and exploitation. He loved and respected the people and was confident that given the chance, they could measure up to that of any in the world.

Newfoundland to the uninformed is a barren, cold, hostile country. It embraces the tenth largest island on earth, together with some 200,000 square miles of an area known as Labrador, on the mainland of Canada. It is recognized as the cradle of white civilization in North America. Settlers derived a living from the seas around the island long before New York, Chicago, Vancouver or Toronto were even dreamed of. Squantum, an Indian who had learned the English language in Newfoundland, surprised the Pilgrim Fathers when they landed at Plymouth Rock, by welcoming them in their own tongue.

In 1927, the ownership of Labrador, which was disputed by Canada, was ceded to Newfoundland by the Privy Council in London. It defined the boundary as starting from the headwaters of all rivers running from the mountain range or height of land of the interior, east to the Atlantic Ocean. This immense area has since proven its worth in the discovery of large iron ore deposits, and more recently uranium, and oil off the coast. Once described by an early explorer as the land God gave to Cain, and by yet another cartographer as being discovered by the English with nothing in it of any value, Labrador may yet prove to be the brightest star in the Dominion.

The land in Newfoundland is largely Crown owned, which simply means that the government owns it. Tracts are leased to pulp and paper mills and oil and gas interests, from which valuable harvests are obtained. Almost one third of the island is covered with lakes and rivers, in which trout and salmon abound. No salmon rivers, as many as two hundred or more, are leased. A former government, which had contemplated leasing, would most certainly have been ousted in the following election had it done so. Its citizens jealously guard the inherent right of access to Crown lands and waters. Denial of this right was brought home to me rather abruptly shortly after my army discharge.

I had been accustomed to resorting to a favourite speckled trout area in the Caledon Hills, forty miles west of Toronto prior to enlisting. Trout fishing has been an obsession of mine since early boyhood, and my first impulse was to visit that particular spot. Imagine my chagrin and disappointment on discovering that the whole area of small ponds and two miles of babbling brooks, fenced and posted. Private fish wardens were everywhere.

I was informed that it had been purchased by a wealthy chain store owner and closed to the public. My thoughts went back to my home province where this would not be tolerated. Nothing daunting, my wife and I decided to try a little stream at a spot near Markham north of Toronto, where we would venture to catch a half dozen brookies for breakfast. Parking our car, we crossed a meadow and proceeded to fish in the very small stream. A shabbily dressed individual carrying a gun approached us, warning us off the property. He informed us that it was now private and he had been assigned to make sure no one fished the stream. It meant of course that we would have to drive almost one hundred miles to the nearest stream, which barely held promise of a modest catch after a long day in practice. I am not presuming that it is illegal to purchase tracts of land under our system of free enterprise, enclosing and excluding the public, but it does indeed leave a mighty sour taste, when one is accustomed to free access to all streams and rivers.

*A Newfoundland Son*

# CHAPTER XIV - BACK TO NEWFOUNDLAND

Yearning to return to Newfoundland, an opportunity arose when in the spring of 1952 an advertisement appeared in a Toronto newspaper, offering Newfoundland government employment to veterinarians. This was being done with the newly formed Veterinary Services Branch of the Department of Agriculture. The area I requested, covered the west coast from Daniel's Harbour to the Codroy Valley, embracing the towns of Cornerbrook and Stephenville. Small farms had been almost forsaken in lieu of more lucrative earnings. Pulp and paper workers at the huge Bowarter Mill, or maintenance staff at the large Stephenville Earnst Harmon Air Force Base, which were to receive subsidies and professional help from the government in re-establishing themselves.

The only dairy herd of any note was that of the large Bowater Corporation in Cornerbrook. It consisted of almost one hundred head of registered Ayrshires imported from Scotland and Canada.

I was accepted for the position and arrived in Cornerbrook with my wife and three small children: Peter, Ralph and Elizabeth. Mr. Warren Dawe, President of the local Agricultural Association, met us. He had created a small farm from a piece of property containing more stones and boulders than I had ever seen. They had been painstakingly gathered and dumped in heaps at the edge of the field. The boulders had been levered out of the ground onto a stone boat made of heavy planking and hauled away by using a small tractor. In spite of the apparent barrenness of the land, it managed to produce the choicest cabbage, turnip and potatoes I ever tasted. In addition to barnyard manure from his small herd, he used kelp and caplin (a small fish that was in abundance during the month of June). Warren worked as superintendent of shipping at Bowaters, and also as head of the Harbour Pilots Association. His wife Edith, a most charming and well-read lady, taught in the local school and even taught some of our children. They had come originally from Port de Grave on the Avalon Peninsula.

I was introduced to nearby farmers and also to Mr. Albert Martin, Manager of the Woodlands Department. Bowaters, at that time, purchased heavy draught horses for woods operations. These they leased or sold to contractors in lots of from five to thirty, depending on the size of the operation. The Newfoundland government agreed to pay me 3,600 dollars per annum, together with a railway pass permitting me to stop any train for transportation as roads were almost non-existent. In addition, I could charge five dollars per call and cover my lodging with an expense account. The latter recalls a rather amusing incident told to me by a small farmer living near the Crabbes River on the west coast.

A certain government representative from the Agriculture Department in St. John's was visiting the area advising farmers on suitable fertilizers. He was very fond of rum, and arriving at the farmer's house, was dying for a drink. His host had two bottles of forty proof, which he had ordered by train, all the way from Cornerbrook. The only hitch was that the government man only had eight dollars cash left to pay for the one man ferry crossing of the Crabbes River, and then by taxi to the railway station where his pass would take him to Cornerbrook. Here he could get a cash advance from the government branch. His host solved the problem by saying he would sign a chit for ten dollars, the cash could be remitted to him when the government man sent in his expense account at the end of the month.

He would sell him the bottle and trust him to send the money at that time, ending by saying that the government had plenty of money and wouldn't miss it. He personally ferried him across the river gratis, his eight dollars intact, and the chit read "To one meal and crossing the Crabbes, twelve dollars." The bottle of rum served to buoy up his spirits on the "Newfy Bullett" the most unforgettable, slowest train ever invented, unfortunately, at the Department's expense. I learned subsequently that this was called padding an expense account, a procedure of which I strongly disapproved.

The road extending from Cornerbrook to Stephenville was simply appalling, full of boulders projecting from its surface and precarious wooden bridges spanning the brooks. It extended for fifty-five miles to the railway terminal, bringing supplies to a road connection with the Harmon Air Base. This stretch of road, twelve miles long, was beautifully paved and maintained by the Americans. It was a delight to drive on it after the bone-shaking trip from Cornerbrook.

My headquarters in Stephenville Crossing was White's Hotel, and there I often met Ralph Tulk, Manager of the Deer Lake Woods Division. He was a great storyteller and one I remember well centered on an emergency medical call he went on with a Dr. Green of Deer Lake. The patient had cut his foot badly while cutting wood with an axe. The man lived in Millertown about forty miles east of Deer Lake, no road; the only connection was by rail. The doctor asked Ralph if he could be taken to the man's home by "Jigger," a small vehicle propelled by hand action or pumping which was used to check the rail when minor mishaps occurred. It was also requisitioned in case of emergencies, such as the one at hand.

Ralph and the doctor started out on a cold November night, taking along a bottle of rum to help ward off the cold. Their way was lighted by a bright full moon, and they sped along until reaching Kitty's Brook, fifteen miles east. Now began a steep grade to Topsails, a railway station on the Long Range Mountains.

In places the grade leveled off where rock cuts had been made, the track proceeding through a hallway with rock walls on either side. At one such place, they were met with what appeared to be the headlight of a train going west. The bottle of rum had half disappeared by this time, and its effect served to accentuate this impression. They immediately rolled off the Jigger and down a steep embankment. The vehicle proceeded on down a slight grade for half a mile where it stopped.

Picking themselves up from the brush and dead grass where they had landed, the two presented a sorry spectacle when they finally crawled on top of the embankment. Peering through the gap, they perceived a bright full moon instead of the anticipated headlight of a train. Walking to the runaway vehicle, they took a good swig, and proceeded on to their destination. They sobered up during the rest of the trip, and in Ralph's words, "by Jingle, the doctor made a pretty good job of the foot."

Roads not capable of accommodating more than a two- wheeled cart drawn by a pony, wound their tortuous way through quaint fishing villages, past rude picket fences enclosing gardens which produced cabbage, turnip and potatoes of unexcelled quality. The fences were durable and strong, providing a bulwark against cattle and sheep that roamed freely through the hamlets in search of pasture.

Life was leisurely in the villages, where most of the activity was centered around the waterfront, where a rich harvest of codfish entered every suitable day. The aroma of salt fish drying in the sun permeated the air during the warm summer months. Neat beds of Asters, Monkshood, Fleur de Lys, and Nasturtiums added a touch of bright colour to the picturesque scene. No roads extended beyond the villages, but rough paths connected the hamlets.

The narrow gauge Newfoundland Railroad provided the only means of travel from the east to the west coast. It skirted deep bays, over barrens and moors, across the Long Range Mountains with peaks two thousand feet high, their names reminding the traveler of a seafaring heritage. Three of the most notable were Main, Mizzen and Gaff Topsail. Once over the "Gaff" the train rolled into the densely wooded valleys and past the great rivers of the west coast. Its final destination being Port-aux-Basque where it connected with the ferry to Cape Breton Island.

Mr. Albert Martin C.E.O. of Bowaters Pulp Mill suggested that I contact the woods operators with a view to supplying a monthly visiting service to the various camps dotted throughout the interior. This, at the rate of one dollar per animal, plus extra for operations was a meager income. I realized, after a few weeks of practice, that the government stipend would be quite inadequate and discussed this with Mr. Dan Gillis, a former Minister of Agriculture in the government, who lived on the west coast in the Highlands.

He operated a small farm and broadcast on the radio a program in native dialect called "Sandy Joe." It dealt with the trials and tribulations of the average fisherman-farmer and was at times most humorous, providing entertainment and information during the lunch hour.

Every evening the residents of fishing villages who were away at distant "woods camps" would listen to a well-known drugstore owner named Gerald S.

Doyle, who sponsored "news from home" on the Island radio. On one occasion the man of the house had gone into an area to cut pulpwood, leaving his wife who had been ill for sometime. At seven sharp that evening, the Doyle's Bulletin came on the air saying, "to Mr. Josh Penny at camp in Hampton (some one hundred and thirty miles distant), from his wife in Cox's Cove. Not getting much better, come home". When read over the radio it came out "Not getting much - Better come home!"

Mr. Gillis did his best and approached those responsible in the government in St. John's, but they were reluctant to increase the salary. Several contractors, the two main ones being, Jim Collier of Gallants and Gus Colbourne of Riverbrook, each having over forty horses, signed up and provided an appreciable boost to my income. I always looked forward to visiting their camps.

Jim would invariably suggest a trouting or bird-hunting jaunt, with Ralph Tulk, when on hand. I would commandeer a Bombardier snowmobile capable of carrying fourteen people, a bottle of spirits, provisions, and would head off to one of the ponds. En route to the fishing area, we would deliver supplies to other camps, and I would make a cursory examination of the horses. Only on rare occasions were my professional services needed.

At times an animal would become impaled on a sharp stick buried in the snow, or come down with Blackwater or pneumonia. Colic was avoided in large measure by simple advice on watering and feeding. Both Jim and Ralph would regale me with stories of humorous incidents occurring over the years.

One such story from Jim was about a trip he made to St. Pierre off the Newfoundland south coast a few years before. Liquor there was cheap and flowing freely. Prior to boarding the boat for the short trip to the mainland again, he purchased four bottles of rum, which he hid about his person. Unfortunately the necks of two bottles protruded prominently from his side pants pockets, a fact which the customs officers were quick to notice on arrival at Grand Bank on the Newfoundland side. They informed Jim, who was about to step off the gangplank, that only one bottle per person was allowed in, duty free, and the rest could not be taken ashore. Jim hurriedly went back on the boat proclaiming that they would be imported legally, and proceeded to consume the contents of three bottles. He was a big, husky man, but no constitution, however robust, could stand such punishment. Shortly after he was taken to a local boarding house waking twenty-eight hours later.

We arrived at the pond, cut holes through the ice, and using bacon rind, tried to attract trout to the surface, often quite successfully. One time Ralph Tulk, ever the prankster, suddenly became very excited and we could clearly see that a fish of unusual proportions was at the end of his line. We hurried over to witness the landing, whereupon he proudly hauled up a bottle of Hudson's Bay rum, which he had, unknown to us, tied on the end of the line. Needless to say, and considering the bitterness of the weather, it was quickly mixed with clear cold water and partly consumed, to the merriment and laughter of the others that had not been so "successful."

The woods camps were invariably made of logs and consisted of a bunkhouse where the men lived. Double bunk beds were arranged along each wall where a wood-burning stove or oil space heater served to provide heat. Clotheslines were strung near the stove from rafters, on which socks, sweaters and other wet clothing were hung to dry at night. The cookhouse was nearby, furnished with plank tables and benches seating about twelve men each. The tables were covered with oilcloth. At the end but part of the same building behind a separate partition, was the kitchen where the cook and cookee slept. One room was reserved for the boss or visiting personalities, such as myself. This area was called the forepeak, analogous to that in the bow of a ship reserved for the crew.

Tasty, satisfying meals were prepared by excellent cooks. Home-baked bread, fish and brewis, boiled dinners, fresh meat usually boiled, heaps of potatoes, with cabbage and turnip was served daily. Meals were usually topped off with bread and molasses or figgy duff. In case the men desired a "mug up" before bedtime tea and coffee were always in good supply. Conversation was rarely permitted during meals, as the work entailed after, doing dishes, mopping the floor and rearranging the tables for the next meal, was considerable, with only one cookee to do this work.

The men ate well and quickly, resorting to their bunkhouse or to the barn to groom the horses afterward. The barns were well removed from the living areas and were built near a brook, the horses being let out for watering at intervals. Fodder and oats were stored in an adjoining shed as were supplies for the men near the kitchen. Drinking water was obtained from the brook, at a point, above where the animals drank, and was taken in wooden barrels to the kitchen. The men worked hard, rising at five o'clock in the morning and working until dark.

Back in the bunkhouse after supper men would sing songs to the accompaniment of the mouth organ or accordion, perhaps indulging in a game of cards, cribbage, or dominos which was very popular. Drinking was not permitted although the odd bottle was smuggled in after a spell at home.

Blackwater or Azoturia was the most serious illness aside from Shipping Fever, which usually affected horses being transported from the mainland during the cold fall weather. Blackwater seemed to strike the animals after a period of inactivity when they would return to work and its onset was very sudden.

On occasion, the horse would collapse on the way home from work right in the middle of the woods road, staying there until it could be moved often in sub-zero weather. A crude shelter somewhat resembling an African grass hut or igloo made of saplings and fir boughs would be erected over the poor animal. Indeed, and at times, it had to be treated in these cramped quarters for a couple of days.

When it was necessary to leave for some remote point at night, I would try to connect with an outgoing freight train, as the road, such as it was, would be drifted in with snow, or impossible to traverse, especially in spring. The freight, with my permit, could be stopped at a point nearest the village or camp, and a snowmobile or horse-drawn sled would take me to the patient. This, I must admit, happened often. My only regret being that the slow-moving train sometimes took twelve to eighteen hours to reach my destination. By this time, the patient had worsened and required two or three days of treatment before responding fully.

The camp was astir at six in the morning, bells on the harnesses tinkling as the horses trotted along the roads winding through a blanket of white, sparkling snow to the cutting and loading area. The pulp logs were hauled to a nearby river bank in readiness for the spring drive to the larger rivers. They would end up in a lake where they finally went to Cornerbrook to satiate the hunger of the giant Bowater Mill, which would process them into paper for the markets of the world. The run-off caused by melting snow provided ample water for the drive, but was of short duration. Men using caulked boots, pike poles and peavies worked quickly and dangerously to untangle the log jams speeding the logs on their way. Often lives were lost when logs piled up into a "Jam" some twenty-feet high then collapsing, burying someone not agile enough to seek the safety of the bank in a hurry. Logs were often left in the retaining lake for most of the summer softening the bark prior to processing.

One event sticks in my mind most vividly. While in St. Anthony, I received a call from Cornerbrook that my veterinary services were required at a woods camp where a horse had been severely injured. Weather reports indicated a severe winter storm in the area of the Belle Isle Straits, some sixty miles west of St. Anthony. When I reached Cook's Harbour, some thirty miles west, the storm in all its fury was dumping snow to a depth of two feet on the unpaved highway. A few miles further on, I encountered an automobile with six passengers hopelessly stuck in a huge snowdrift. They had shut all the windows and left the engine running. I immediately stopped my pickup and warned them to open the windows, as, one or two inside were already showing signs of drowsiness. Fortunately, a large Army four-wheel drive appeared out of drifting snow. They were trying to reach the St. Anthony Meteorology Base, an American Unit established as a defence post during the war. They managed to squeeze two of the women passengers into the cab and said that if they reached St. Anthony, would send out an Army snowmobile to rescue the remaining four passengers. I later learned that everything went well - they were rescued.

I finally decided to try to make Big Brook, a small fishing community about eight miles in distance, before the drifting snow blocked the road entirely before dark. Darkness was beginning to descend, so with great difficulty, forcing my way through deep drifts, I decided to walk the remaining eight miles. I could hear the incessant crashing of ice pans against the shoreline merely a few yards away. After plodding along in total darkness, finding my way by probing the edge of the road, I finally saw through the drifting snow, the lights of Big Brook. Knocking at the door of a well-lit house, I was welcomed into the warm interior by Eric McLean and his wife. They were astounded at the apparition covered with a half inch of snow and ice which had frozen to my face and clothing.

Strong gusts of wind would periodically shake the two-story wood building, which was heated by a wood-burning kitchen stove, and an oil-burning unit on the upstairs landing. Big Brook had no telephones, or other means of communication with the outside world. The following day, having no news of my whereabouts, the R.C.M.P. in Cornerbrook dispatched a helicopter to the area and reported seeing a pickup truck and car embedded in a snowdrift sixteen miles from Big Brook. Three days later, snowploughs broke through to Big Brook and managed to pass the word along that I was alive and well. The road crews drove my pickup to me and thankfully I proceeded to Cornerbrook.

*Nathan Budgell, DVM*

# CHAPTER XV - NIAGARA FALLS

At the end of my two-year contract in Newfoundland with the government, I concluded that it was impossible to sustain the expense of that type of practice. I purchased a Land Rover, but even that sturdy vehicle could not stand up to the deplorable road conditions. Maintaining the essential repairs, with the subsidy of eight cents a mile, was too little. As a consequence, I approached the Department with the view to increasing both my salary and travel allowance. They discussed the matter, but decided they could do nothing at that time. Sharrie and I decided to return to the mainland, in this case, Ontario. I did enjoy my brief two-year stay in Newfoundland, and grew to love and respect the people who were very appreciative and understanding. Most of them were related and the young folks addressed their elders as Uncle or Aunt, which I thought a rather endearing term.

In Niagara Falls, I looked up a friend who owned and operated a canvas goods manufacturing plant, making everything from tents, to gloves, to awnings. He stayed with me on a successful moose-hunting trip and gladly offered me a position with his firm. The idea rather intrigued me, after the exhausting routine of being on call at almost every minute of the day and night the whole week long.

Being at loose ends and needing to provide for a family of three, I decided that it might be to my advantage to acquire knowledge of the sales industry. I accepted a position as sales manager. After all, what was there to lose? I could still practice in the event the new venture did not turn out.

Not realizing how intricate and competitive the business of manufacturing and selling was, I ate, slept and drank awnings, tents, gloves and tarpaulins for twenty-four hours a day. Little time was spent with my family; holidays and weekends off, were unknown. The owner insisted I drive around summer resorts with a large painted sign in my car window, advertising awnings and giving a sales pitch to anyone who seemed interested. If such was the case, I would proceed to their cottage, and measure the windows clinching a contract whenever possible.

Of course selling an order to a large factory needing new awnings was ideal, as therein lay a sizable net profit. It seemed that some competitor would always come up with a better glove or awning, and the whole recycling of ideas to make an improvement began all over again. Gloves with special steel staples for handling metal products, asbestos gloves for hot materials, leather gloves; canvas, aluminum and fiberglass awnings; and other goods which might give us an edge in a certain area were constantly improved upon. I could not possibly see how a better product was possible.

Competitors violated every rule in the book to capture a large account, which would bring in repeat orders, gaining a steady sales volume. I could not see that their product was any better, or their means of supply, but perhaps the new sales manager was a good friend of the salesman or his sales manager. I found myself trying by every means to offset their attempts, but after two years became tired of the rat race, and told my friend I would rather go back to my own profession. He was quite upset and pleaded with me to stay, saying that some of the new large accounts I had brought in might be lost. I visited them all and explained that I would be resigning, which I did two months later.

I always hoped that the Newfoundland government would revamp its plan for veterinarians, as none had been employed subsequent to my leaving. It was rumoured that a separate branch was to be set up, more or less, independently of the Agriculture Branch. In the interim, I applied and was given a position with the Health of Animals Branch with the federal government.

Sharrie presented us with twins in Niagara Falls whom we named John David and Daphne Christine. They were very much loved and admired by a doting grandmother who never failed to be with them at every opportunity. We were still living in Niagara Falls, and since my work was in Toronto at the Swift Canadian Plant, I could only be with them on weekends, leaving Sharrie with quite a load of work. Fortunately we brought a young lady back with us from Newfoundland. Her name was Francis and she stayed to help during the time when the twins were young, helping to alleviate some of the work.

On weekends I took over some of the chores, especially night feedings, and became involved in some amusing, though rather unorthodox procedures. One night the yelling of two hungry mouths at exactly three o'clock in the morning awakened me. I had been told that it was most important to sterilize the bottles for each baby, and to make sure that each was fed from its own. Formula had been made up and left in the fridge, but the contents had to be warmed prior to feeding, and one baby took stronger milk than the other did. This of course took a few minutes and in the meantime, there was enough noise being created to wake the dead. I put one bottle in the single electric warmer, and when ready, hurriedly stuck it in one mouth. The other seemed to think I was playing favorites and increased its yelling tenfold. Throwing caution and convention to the wind, I put two bawling babies on one arm and proceeded to insert the nipple first in one mouth and then the other, while the second bottle was heating. The noise subsided, but started up again when I transferred the bottle. I could think of no other alternative and imagine my surprise when I turned to find my wife standing aghast in the doorway watching the whole procedure. When our eyes met, she burst out laughing, and came to my aid.

We bought a double warmer next day, the twins evidencing no ill effects. They were a delight to observe and their sister Libby adored them, being almost motherly in her attendance at only age three.

It comes to my mind that it was Libby at this age who one night when my wife and I were getting ready to go to a dance answered the telephone. We could hear her say from our bedroom, "I'm very sorry, Dr. Budgell cannot come to the phone at present, he's busy in the bedroom with my mother."

## CHAPTER XVI - HAMMOND FARM

An opportunity came, once again, to change our lives. The situation, after eighteen long months, came one day when I received a phone call from an official of the Bowaters Newfoundland Pulp & Paper Mill Ltd., in Cornerbrook, asking if I would be interested in leasing their farm and purchasing the stock and equipment. The official was a very close friend of ours. Having seen the herd, I knew it to be of excellent stock and fully accredited. The proposal was fifty thousand dollars for the herd and equipment, and an annual lease of ten thousand dollars for the land and buildings. I flew down to Cornerbrook and met the management of Bowaters to obtain further details and examine the accounts.

I found that the farm operation showed a net loss of eight thousand dollars on its milk sales, down sixteen hundred dollars from the year before. I concluded that the milk production, alone, could not help but lose in view of the feed and other costs, but that if a market for the sale of young stock could be built up, it could quite conceivably be a profitable venture. Many breeders in the U.S.A. and Canada would no doubt be glad to acquire some of this great Hammond herd. In addition, diversification in the form of egg production and beef, to supply the local market, was a distinct possibility. I promised to let Bowaters know, as soon as possible. For some strange reason, they expressed a desire that I not visit the farm until my decision for, or against, was finalized.

In the meantime, I contacted the London, England office saying I thought the purchase price rather high, but received a negative response. It was later revealed to me that the reason for not wanting me to inspect the stock and equipment was that the manager, at the time, would thoroughly disapprove of the transaction. I could easily understand his attitude as he had worked for many years to bring it to its present level. The land literally had to be cleared out of the forest, stock purchased and breeding carefully regulated. The company did not expand the farm into exporting young breeding stock, because they were mainly interested in supplying milk to Cornerbrook, a "Company" town.

The annual visit of Sir Eric Bowater was a gala occasion. One might have thought that royalty was arriving. Houses were painted, hedges neatly trimmed and a welcoming committee erected a huge tent on the lawn of Strawberry Hill, his official residence about twelve miles from the town. Invited guests regaled themselves and listened to his address on the state of the economy and the mill in particular. The Union Jack was proudly flown from a tall mast in the center of the town, symbol of Britain's interest in its oldest colony.

My wife did not agree with my acceptance of the terms, feeling the government job provided security we could count on. However, we pulled up stakes and once again headed for Cornerbrook staying in the local inn, while arrangements were made for the reluctant manager to leave the farm. He refused to vacate his house leaving his furniture in it, and headed for the mainland where he stayed for almost three months. We were forced to occupy a small two-room building on the farm during this time.

A few days after paying the lease and making a substantial down payment on the herd, I noticed four cows isolated in a small pasture near the barn. Asking the herdsman why they were there, he informed me that they were reactors to the Brucellosis test, or contagious abortion. This disease, a highly infectious one, caused cows to abort their calves prematurely, and was dreaded by all breeders.

I was stunned and contacted the Manager at Bowaters who informed me that they were not aware of the condition because the farm manager alone had control over all those matters. I immediately contacted the Federal District Veterinarian in St. John's, a classmate of mine, and he informed me of the situation. No one at Bowaters had revealed the presence of the disease, and the farm manager, of course, would not talk with me. It was something that could mean the difference between success and failure, as no stock could leave the farm until the disease had been eradicated. Calves had been vaccinated regularly by the veterinarian with "Strain Nineteen," a proven preventative, but somehow the bacillus had gained access to the premises. No actual cases of abortion had occurred, but blood tests supported a questionable condition.

I immediately ordered the slaughter of the five animals, hoping that it might help with strict sanitary precautions to control or eliminate the disease. Three months later the tests revealed questionable reactions in two young heifers. This pattern went on and two years later I was paid a visit by top veterinarians of the Health of Animals Branch in Ottawa. They seemed perplexed by the fact that this questionable reaction showed with every test, but with no abortions occurring. Another peculiar fact was that only young heifers showed a questionable reaction. This seemingly harmless situation, as it may appear to the layman, prevented me from selling any stock, except for beef, and at a fraction of the actual value. Bowaters showed little sympathy, not realizing fully the implications of a Brucellosis-infected herd.

Milk production was the only source of income, and a losing one at that. In a climate renowned for its fickleness, haymaking became a desperate gamble with the weather. In some years, the whole crop would be almost unfit for feed, as it would loose its quality by not being properly dried. Ensilage from grass and kale helped offset this, but hay had to be imported from the mainland, at a rather staggering cost. After a couple of years the Brucellosis problem lingered on so I decided to diversify into the egg market. Eggs coming in from Nova Scotia were subjected to a terrific amount of jolting and breakage on the railway. Often the quality was reduced through shipping delays.

**Figure 18 Gerald Boyle, George Metcalf, Stuart Burton with Art Ivany driving the tractor.**

    I decided to convert a large barn previously used to house young stock into a hennery. Following this, I imported ten thousand baby chicks and five thousand laying hens, but realized that eventually a modern fully mechanized unit was the only answer to offset the intense competition from the mainland producers. The Trans Canada Highway was being rapidly constructed from St. John's to Port-aux-Basques and would be finished in a year or so. This would enable truckers to bring in eggs directly over a paved road, cutting down on breakage and spoilage.

    In addition to the hennery, I built a grading station and a small killing plant to take care of the old hens. The flock increased to twenty thousand birds. Everything seemed to be going well, eggs produced one day, made their way to the tables in Cornerbrook the next day. In the meantime, producers in St. John's were building up their production at a great rate, and formed the Newfoundland Poultry Producer's Association to promote sales. They landed their product in our area from flocks of up to 150,000 layers, and in the face of this competition, the Nova Scotian producers sold their eggs at rock-bottom prices hoping to retain what had been a very lucrative market.

    The highway was completed a year later, and almost daily large transports from the mainland and St. John's could be seen entering Cornerbrook. I could no longer advertize strictly fresh eggs, and Canada Packers, my distributor, could no longer accord me the five- to ten-cent margin I enjoyed. Shiploads of feed were brought into St. John's at a much lower cost than by the rail, which I was obliged to use. To make matters worse, milk from the Truro Milkshed was also being trucked in. Prices dropped, but the feed costs and labour kept going up. Even farm labour was demanding parity with mill workers, some of the highest paid in eastern Canada.

Two years after taking over the farm, and with the help of a few interested citizens, we started the West Newfoundland Agricultural Fair Association. We hoped that by doing so, we could arouse a greater interest in local farm products, including handicrafts. This effort was not without some amusing incidents.

The government allocated prize money to winners and at times there were not enough exhibits in a certain class to warrant distribution of money available. A poultry judge had been sent from the Agriculture Department in St. John's to judge both these and other classes, such as horses, cattle and other livestock.

An enthusiast from across the Bay, brought a couple of Rhode Island hens to the fair, with two pigeons, putting them in a vacant cage. The poultry class was not very large and the judge, accustomed to having a few swigs of strong stuff from breakfast on, arrived late for judging, but in a very jovial mood. He looked over the birds with great intent and awarded first prize in its class to a fine pair of Peking ducks. I had never seen pigeons transformed into ducks with such rapidity. The judge remarked that the money was there to be given away anyway, and the poor woman took enough trouble to bring them along.

Later in the afternoon, horses were being judged and the only available space was at our farm. About six were entered, not nearly enough to absorb the money allocated. I quickly sent one of the farm hands up the road to a neighbour named Abe Carter, to have him bring his horse over. The poor animal, much the worse for wear after years of hard work in the woods and on Abe's small farm, came hobbling through the gate. Its one blind eye had turned white and stood out very prominently against the dark colour of its coat. It was paraded down the center aisle of the building before the judge, who had fortified himself with a few extra rounds, was in an ever-more jovial and buoyant mood. He looked at the frame of skin and bones, remarking that it was a fine-looking beast worthy of the first prize of twenty dollars. Furthermore, he awarded it another twenty dollars for best in the working class. Abe Carter was of course delighted having earned, together with his other exhibits of farm produce, a total of sixty dollars for the day.

The annual Fair was eagerly anticipated, although getting enough people to participate was indeed a chore. I spent endless days and nights visiting farmers and families in the rural areas, imploring them to show the best of their handicrafts, jams, cooking and farm stock. They felt, but not in all cases, that they were much too busy, but once they started to move, became quite eager.

I started the Hammond Farm Four "H" Club, and in the inter-club meetings with others on the west coast, helped to stimulate interest on behalf of the elders. For three years in succession, the clubs exhibited their work in several booths at one end of the arena. A lot of effort went into asking citizens of Cornerbrook to put up one or two Four-H'ers for a day or two and I must confess that the good people did not fall short. They opened their hearts to the youngsters who enjoyed every moment of their stay.

We were living in a dwelling owned by Bowaters Company during this period of time. It had seven large rooms and was built on a knoll commanding a magnificent view of the majestic Humber Valley, through which flowed the beautiful Humber River, world renowned for its famous salmon fishing. Sportsmen from almost every corner of the globe, from Earls and Dukes to the humble natives tried their luck on the river, most of them very successfully. As Peter and Ralph grew older, they too, rods in hand, frequented the river especially in the evening. From our house we could hear their shrill shout of exultation when they hooked a beauty of eight to twelve pounds. Trout were in abundance in the numerous small streams, which emptied into the river. It was not unusual for the boys, accompanied by their sister Libby and the twins David and Daphne, to meander away before breakfast and bring home a dozen or two brookies, which soon found their way into the frying pan.

A few yards from the house was a barn used by the original occupant to house a few cattle and hens. It had been unused for a long time, but was in a good state of repair. I converted the spacious loft into a Four-H clubroom, and used it for meetings and other activities. Our Club grew to a membership of thirty, many of whom enjoyed trips to Ottawa or St. John's as a result of winning in various Four-H projects. The coordinator for Newfoundland was a Mr. David Malcolm, who would visit the west coast frequently to advise and encourage the clubs. He was well suited for the job and well liked by the youngsters.

Peter and Ralph, assumed a share of the farm work such as mowing hay, driving trucks and tractors as they grew older. It was not unusual to find them on a tractor at seven o'clock in the morning, during hay time, where they stayed until dark. Next day, they would drive the hay baler then transport the bales to the barn for storage.

The boys thoroughly enjoyed trips to the wood camps on weekends. Ralph had a voracious appetite which did not diminish at home, but Peter was a rather fastidious eater, even to the point of eating his meals while sitting on the cellar steps, for fear of the food being contaminated by the breath of the others sitting around the table. When visiting the camps, the psychological block disappeared entirely, and his appetite was nothing short of ravenous. Whether it was because he saw the hard-working men doing justice to a huge meal without hesitation, I do not know, but it was a pleasure to see him eating to his heart's content. The men were delighted to have them around, taking them into the wood-cutting areas by horse-drawn sled.

Most of the workers wore a boot called a Logan, made of leather uppers with rubber at the foot end. In addition, they wore heavy wool windbreakers, an outfit very much envied by both Peter and Ralph, who did not rest until I had equipped them with those items.

Many stories of tragic happenings involving members of hunting and fishing parties were commonplace. These could be accepted when fishermen pursuing their livelihood were caught in severe storms at sea, but when experienced sportsmen and guides were the victims, the cause always remained a mystery. Two instances remain vividly in my memory.

Three American servicemen and two Newfoundland guides set out from Glover Island in Grand Lake where the U.S. Army had a hunting and fishing camp. They stowed equipment and food in a large canoe and paddled the short distance to the mainland where they climbed the range of hills in search of caribou and moose. They were to return before dark, and when they failed to do so, the others at the camp concluded that they had taken along a tent and camped for the night.

Next afternoon, there was still no sign of the party, and three others from the island went in search. Arriving at the trails beginning, they found no sign of the canoe. Becoming alarmed, they hurried back to Glover Island and sent an urgent message to the Harmon Air Force Base, at Stephenville, asking for help. In a matter of minutes, helicopters and planes were scouring the wilderness to no avail. Early next day the search continued and thereafter for several days, but no sign of the five, including their equipment, was ever found. It was afterward learned that the men were wearing thigh rubbers to navigate the many bogs and brooks. This with heavy clothing, probably caused them to go rapidly to the bottom of Grand Lake, one of the largest and deepest in the country, if, as was supposed, the canoe overturned. The most mystifying outcome was that no vestige of wearing apparel, or other articles, was ever found.

On another occasion, the manager of one of the local hotels Erick Johnson, and his friend Max Rabbits, also an expert outdoorsman, went fishing for trout in Serpentine Lake, twenty-five miles from Cornerbrook. The weather was good, but the body of water nestling between high mountains was subject to violent squalls. They had taken a sturdy canoe to navigate the river leading from the lake to the sea. When they failed to return that night, people naturally concluded that they had decided to take shelter in a small cabin near the river's exit. Next day a party of sportsmen going to the Bowaters Camp, about ten miles down the river, came upon their overturned canoe. They searched in vain for survivors, and dragging by the R.C.M.P. brought no results. Their bodies were never found, and so another unsolved mystery was filed in the record of unexplainable tragedies.

*A Newfoundland Son*

    Work on the farm was also not without its near tragedies. Once while unloading sacks of grain from the railway car at the farm siding into the storage building by truck, our son Ralph, who was on top of the load, was crushed between the top frame of the doorway into which the truck was backing. Loud yells to the driver by other workers caused him to stop, but not until Ralph had been crushed severely, necessitating four days in hospital. Being young and resilient, he recovered within three months without any apparent ill effects.

    The children, as they grew, enjoyed appearing on a television program during the Children's Hour called Kiddies Corner. They would take guinea hens, rabbits, lambs, baby chicks, and even piglets with them to give atmosphere to some of the programs. Libby and Daphne also participated in the Children's Little Theatre, under the direction of Frank Gronich. Libby won the best actress award one year and Daphne excelled in the production of Rumple Stiltskin. David, her twin, loved to sing and at that tender age had a certain quality in his voice which his mother firmly believed would bring him singing fame.

    Peter and Ralph were entered into King's College School at Windsor, Nova Scotia. There under the able guidance of Mr. John Derrick and staff, acquired a good grounding in scholastics, including sports and cadet training under a Regimental Sergeant Major named Finny which fitted them well for later life. The ironic thing was that Mr. Finny was a sergeant in the army, at my camp in Toronto, years before.

**Figure 19 My Mother, Susan (Langford Budgell Critch) Oxford with me in the farmhouse at Hammond's Farm.**

During my ten years on the farm, I had ventured into quaint little outports, where the people pursued their daily rounds and common tasks, much as they had over the past five hundred years. They fished in summer, keeping ample by salting for winter use, and picked berries of all varieties in abundance, preserving them into jams. They shot quantities of sea birds, geese and partridge, also preserving many of them with salt in barrels. They harvested delicious turnips, potatoes and cabbage, and had their flavor enhanced by the use of rich kelp and added fish fertilizer, and then stored them in sod-covered houses called root cellars. No tastier meal was to be enjoyed anywhere than a "Jiggs" dinner. It consisted of salt beef, ample slices of turnip, cabbage, potatoes, carrots and parsnip, over which was poured the juice or "likker" from the boiling.

*A Newfoundland Son*

Beef or mutton during the winter, supplemented their diets. Beef meant exactly what its name implied, simply the flesh of a bovine. No such cuts as sirloin, rump or T-bone were known. One went into the outer storeroom, where sub-freezing temperatures kept the meat in excellent condition. One would carve off a portion of the carcass where it often went into the pot along with a piece of "salt," helping to add a special flavour to the appetizing meal. The host would say "would you like a bit of fresh, or a piece of salt". Peas puddin, made of yellow split peas boiled in a cloth until mushy, and figgy duff, made of suet, flour and currants, were served in generous slices with each meal.

No clothing could be warmer than that knitted from homespun wool on knitting needles often made of wood or bone. There was also no warmer welcome afforded anyone entering the home than that shown by these kindly people. They seemed to delight in the sharing of their hospitality.

Food supplies became very depleted in early spring, and a spirit of restlessness pervaded the many hamlets along the coast. Perhaps it was due to the isolation of a long winter, followed by the stirring of the arctic ice mass on its relentless way south, urged on by the icy Labrador current, bearing its myriad of seals. Anticipation of a plentiful harvest providing fresh meat, skins for clothing, oil and fat for commerce, awakened in these hardy individuals, a sense of adventure, and desire to go to the "Front," as the hunt was spoken of, fearless in the face of imminent danger at every outcome.

**Figure 20 A great Thanksgiving feast with the whole family.**

Life on the farm was not without its amusing incidents. However, in retrospect many could well have ended in tragedy. Ayrshire cattle are very temperamental and on occasion have to be handled adroitly, especially those with long horns. One time we missed one of the cows that we knew to be in calf. Jack Bonnell the herdsman, and I proceeded to an outlying field in the jeep, conducting a search. I had taken along my black medical bag containing essential supplies in case of calving difficulties.

We located the cow by a clump of trees, while she was in the process of calving. She was experiencing difficulty with the birth as the calf was partially born. Tying a hitch around her horns, we secured her to a tree and shortly after we delivered a fine healthy bull calf. We released her head and were about to put the calf in the jeep and head for the barn, when the cow suddenly ran amok.

With bloodcurdling roars and snorts she headed straight in my direction. I turned to run, a quick glance over my shoulder revealed the most dreadful pair of sharp horns, near my posterior. A birch tree, which had been blown over by the wind, afforded my only hope of escape. I reached it in jig time, leaping to a point about five feet from the ground, holding on for dear life. The beast being foiled of her prey threw huge pieces of ground into the air with her front hooves. Looking around, she spied my black bag and probably thinking it was a dog, tossed it several times into the air.

Jack Bonnell, in the meantime, tried to retrieve it, whereupon she headed in his direction. His only hope of escape was to run backward up a small incline in the direction of the jeep. Seeing his predicament, I hurriedly descended from my perch grabbed a stout stick, and proceeded to poke and hit the animal on the nose whenever the chance arose, meanwhile urging Jack to get the calf into the jeep as quickly as possible. This he did with great dexterity, and as soon as the mother heard the bawling of her baby in the confined space, she immediately became very docile, following the vehicle slowly to the barn. This incident substantiated the stories I had heard and read about the breed.

**Figure 21 Ralph and Libby on the fence with David below them.**

Incidents at the farm resulted, at times, in fatal and near fatal outcomes. Our neighbour Don Sharpe had cleared some land about one and a half miles away, on the opposite side of the Humber River. In fall and spring, due to sudden storms, the river could make crossing very treacherous. He built and operated a small abattoir to slaughter beef cattle. After processing, they were delivered, along with other commodities, to various communities on the north and east coasts. He would buy young stock in the spring, fatten them on lush pastures and slaughter them when the weather turned cold. The one and most dangerous procedure was crossing the Humber River on a homemade raft in inclement weather.

Nathan Budgell, DVM

One afternoon in late November, when almost a foot of snow had already fallen, and ice had accumulated on the riverbank, we received an urgent call from the farmer's wife, Lilley. She had called to say her husband had left the opposite bank with five cattle on a rather crude raft or skow, and she was very worried. A strong wind and blinding snowstorm had sprung up obliterating everything in sight. Our two boats that we used on the river in summer were safely stored in our barn loft. We knew that the raft and its occupants could easily be carried down river by the current into the "Devil's Dancing Pool," where the river tumbled through a very narrow gorge. The raft could easily be upset on submerged rocks possibly with the total loss of life.

There was nothing else to do of course but get our boat from the barn loft, drag it over the snow-covered fields, down the river bank and put it into the swiftly moving current. Eliciting the help of George Metcalf, our foreman, a man as tough as nails, and another assistant, Stuart Burton, who knew every inch of the river, we paddled furiously to find the skow. We finally found it at a bend about one mile down river, where the water rushed furiously into an eddy spinning the skow round and round. Throwing a rope to the poor farmer who, by this time, was almost too cold to move, and with the storm increasing in intent, we managed to inch the raft against the current to a safe landing several yards from the man's residence. The water had frozen his clothing making every movement comparable to that of one in a rusty suit of armor. The cattle seemed none the worse for their ordeal and soon recovered in a warm pen.

The farmer's wife who had been anxiously waiting on the riverbank thanked us profusely for avoiding what could have been a tragic ending. It was ironic that a year or two later, the farmer's eighteen-year-old son, Larry, was crossing the same area in a motor boat, somehow fell out and drowned. He was unable to extricate himself from the motor and was clipped by the propeller.

Another time when the district veterinarian was visiting the farm testing blood in some of the stock, he inadvertently turned his back on a large bull in a pen adjoining our calf pens. The space between the bars allowed the animal to extend his horns about halfway across the aisle. Without warning, he lifted the vet gently by the crotch, elevating him to the ceiling then as quietly, lowered him down again to the floor. Being held in such an uncompromising position, caused the unfortunate man to turn ashen with fright, but afraid to yell for fear of infuriating the bull. I did not actually witness the incident, but heard of it second hand. The vet, Dr. Button, was too embarrassed to reveal the ordeal to me personally.

One other time my wife decided that she would help improve the appearance of the yard by burning dead grass left over from the fall before. The burn was started in the morning, but she did not realize it extended through a fence containing flammable young birch. Seeing the situation was getting out of hand, she yelled to Peter, our son, who came running with a rake, pulling the burning stalks away from the fence as fast as possible. Meanwhile, she phoned the farm some three-quarters of a mile distant to summon men with portable fire extinguishers and the Cornerbrook fire department some fifteen miles away. The farm hands arrived, with not a moment to spare, as Peter was fast losing his capacity to contain the fire. The fire sirens could be heard for miles rushing up the road. By the time they arrived, the blaze was practically extinguished, and the men amused themselves by squirting water at one another through the haze of smoke. The firemen felt rather abashed at having to come fifteen miles to the scene of action, but took it all in good spirits. This was much to the relief of my wife who felt somewhat embarrassed, especially when one of the men said "What's wrong, Mrs. Budgell, things a little quiet here?"

Peter and Ralph became very proficient in marksmanship, spending many happy hours shooting rats in a dump some distance from the farm. Once, on his way to school, Ralph shot a beautiful red fox crossing a farm field, and dressed the skin, which he proudly presented to his mother in the form of a neckpiece that she wore for several years. On another day in the fall, the boys treed a black bear, which they also dressed out and used as a floor rug for some years.

About two years before leaving the farm, I purchased a small herd of Holstein cows from the Grenfell Mission farm in St. Anthony. During the few trips to negotiate the sale, I had occasion to visit the final resting place of Sir Wilfred and Lady Grenfell, and also that of Dr. John Mason Little, whose ashes were interred in a large boulder behind the Tea House overlooking the town of St. Anthony. How proud they would have been to view the modern hospital, which is said to be one of the finest in eastern Canada.

One cannot measure the unselfish devotion and dedication, which went into the completion of the Grenfell dream after many years of toil. Very little of that spirit remains today, and this was emphasized by a remark made to me by a prominent official of the Mission, to the effect, that the spirit which motivated Sir Wilfred was as "dead as a doornail".

In 1967, while carrying a hind of beef from our slaughterhouse, I ruptured a disk in my back, which left me totally unable to maneuver. On the advice of Dr. Bill Dewer of Toronto visiting us at the farm, I flew to the Toronto General Hospital for an operation. Dr. Dewar did a splendid job replacing the disk, but I unfortunately developed a clot in my left leg a few days later, causing me to hover between life and death. I was too stubborn to die, and a month later, at the end of August, flew back to Cornerbrook accompanied by my son Ralph, my back reinforced by a steel pin.

Recovery was fairly rapid, and I was pleased to learn that while away, my son Peter had assumed complete responsibility, directing the men in their various tasks, and, himself carrying out monumental tasks which I never thought possible due to his age. He arose pretty well before dawn and had the men's vehicles all gassed up for the day's work when they arrived.

The following year, due to the increased cost of labour, stiff competition from mainland egg producers, who could readily transport their goods on the newly paved highways at a cost far below mine, I decided to give up the business of farming. While negotiating the sale of stock and equipment, much against my will in 1968, I reapplied for a position with the Health of Animals Branch in meat inspection. I was accepted and moved to Prince Edward Island as Assistant Veterinarian in Charge. Proceeds from the sale of farm holdings were hardly enough to cover outstanding bills, and much of the machinery had to be sold at a bare minimum. The thought of having to spend day after day incising glands and intestines once again was anathema to me, having spent ten years largely in the great outdoors, in an unrestricted environment.

My family had enjoyed every minute on the farm and I knew full well that they would always treasure the experience. Peter, to help out, obtained a job with a local dairy when not in school. Ralph worked as a bouncer in a nightclub. He had at that age attained a height of six feet three inches and weighed one hundred and eighty pounds and proved to be an excellent bouncer.

After eighteen months at Canada Packers, I was informed that a Japanese Whaling Company intended to repair and operate a defunct Norwegian station at Williamsport on the north east coast of the Great Northern Peninsula of Newfoundland. The whale meat would be processed and shipped to Japan where it formed a staple source of protein in the Japanese diet for centuries.

Whale meat, to the Japanese, was as important as beef to the people of Europe and North America. From the carcass was extracted oil to heat the lamps of the world before the advent of electricity. From the bones were made combs, girdle supports and knitting needles and a gland in the nostrils supplied scent for perfumes. In fact, everything from soap to cooking and heating oil was derived from this great mammal.

Intensive hunting decimated their numbers to such an extent that an International Whaling Commission was set up to establish quotas. Canada permitted limited taking of whales until 1968, with the quota at Williamsport being two to three hundred of the Finback variety. In addition to Williamsport, two other stations were operated, one at Dildo, Newfoundland, and one at Port Blandford, Nova Scotia. These two engaged in the taking mainly of Sei whales, a smaller variety.

Whale flesh, though generally referred to as meat in most countries, was classed as fish in Japan, coming as it did from the ocean. It was classed as a meat product in Canada and, as such, was subject to the rules and regulations of the Meat Inspection Act under the supervision of Veterinary Meat Inspectors. The establishment at Williamsport was called the Atlantic Whaling Company, and to our department was known as W.I.

## CHAPTER XVII - WHALING

The Whaling Station was located in a deep fiord, some seven miles inland surrounded by towering mountains. A salmon river, with an abundance of deep enticing pools, emptied into the extremity of the fiord. In the immediate vicinity of the station, a trout stream emptied its clear water into the inlet. Some of this water was contained in a dam to supply pure water for washing the whale meat, and drinking water for the staff.

The east coast of the Great Northern Peninsula remains as yet an unspoiled wilderness. Sparkling water cascades down every valley from crystal-clear ponds nestling like diamonds high in the mountains, their surface reflecting fleecy white clouds drifting across an azure blue sky. In their depths lie thousands of trout which find their way to the lowland streams meandering through verdant small valleys, providing hours of enjoyment for young barefoot boys navigating the brooks in search of that elusive big one.

How often, in my later years, did I go back in memory to boyhood days. Sitting on the banks of a quiet stream trying to recapture the exhilaration of moments spent alone on the trail of a cagey old trout, until that final moment of conquest. Such idyllic freedom and peace was to be found in Williamsport, far removed from the din of traffic and noise of industry. The only comparable roar was that of huge waves expending themselves on granite cliffs, or perhaps the distant, subdued noise of a waterfall.

The executive staff at the station consisted of seven Japanese, most of whom were graduates of the Tokyo Marine College. They were in the charge of E. Terrada, a very able administrator. In addition, there were twenty local workers, mainly from nearby Englee or Roddicton. To help break the monotony and add a little spice, twelve young girls were employed to pack the whale meat. Some invariably had the distinction of presenting the community with a half-Japanese or pure-Newfoundland bairn during the following winter. Nothing daunting, however, they were always ready to return the following summer.

The Health of Animals Staff, and the Department of Fisheries were housed in a building nearby. Mrs. Randall, wife of the Foreman, Mr. Les Randall, did the housekeeping chores. Meals were simple, but always ample, and the kettle was boiling at all hours, so that anyone could have a cup of tea or coffee with home-made bread, jam or cakes. Cribbage was very much in vogue during the off hours and another game called forty-fives was quite popular.

The equipment had deteriorated somewhat, not having been used or serviced for sometime. With excellent co-operation from the Japanese, it was brought up to acceptable standards. I came to admire the Japanese greatly for their cleanliness and ingenuity.

**Figure 22 The Whaling Ship "Fumi."**

The whaling ship "Fumi," of 180 tons, was used to hunt to a distance of 190 miles off the coast. Operations usually began in early June in waters festooned with huge icebergs and masses of floating ice pans, ending in November when freezing temperatures made living and working conditions unbearable. I had occasion to make several trips on the Fumi, and although saddened by the killing of these huge, gentle creatures, enjoyed steaming through the iceberg fields studying the myriad of birds and animals making up the marine environment.

Flotsam, consisting of grapefruit, plastic bottles, empty lemon dispensers, catalogues and an assortment of other food and nonperishable items were found everywhere. This caused much chagrin in the fishermen whose nets were befouled by masses of this garbage floating along the coast.

Plankton, made up of large quantities of small marine shellfish, sea lice, and vegetable matter floated on the surface of the ocean, making up the greater part of the diet of whales. In the northern climes, caplins in the millions, provide an additional supplement.

Most of the whales caught in June and July at Williamsport were engorged with this small fish. At one point a net tightly enmeshed in the baleen of a whale, had prevented the poor creature from swallowing food causing it to become very emaciated. On another occasion, we recovered three thick Eaton's catalogues from the stomach of a whale.

The blue whale is the world's largest mammal attaining a length of over one hundred feet and a weight of up to ninety tons, with the Finback ranking a close second. They are a setaceous mammal of fishlike form, one of the larger pelagic species but distinguishable from dolphins and porpoises. Whales have the forelimbs developed as broad, flattened paddles and the hind limbs are absent. They also have a thick layer of blubber immediately beneath the skin. The whalebone type is toothless, while others such as the sperm and right whale have teeth.

**Figure 23 Finback whale as seen from the deck of the "Fumi."**

Daily, the whaling ship Fumi put to sea at about dusk, after the whales, usually two, had been processed. The object was to arrive at the hunting grounds by dawn. One of the crew, usually Japanese, ascended into the lookout, or crowsnest, a barrel-like structure at the top of the foremast. Telephone communication was maintained between the lookout and the captain, and when a pod of whales was sighted, intense excitement rippled throughout the whole ship. The captain navigated the ship to within a distance of about one hundred feet of the huge creatures, and at an opportune moment, handed the wheel over to his mate, manning the harpoon gun located in the bow.

A well-directed shot sent the harpoon, weighing some one hundred pounds, into the chest cavity where three barbed hooks, previously tied parallel to the shaft, were released into a lateral position. The harpoon was attached to a two-inch nylon rope which, in turn, was wound around a winch operated by steam. The whale, after being hit, immediately dived to a depth of five hundred feet or more and the winch either took in the slack, or let more rope out whenever needed. The struggle continued some times close to three-quarters of an hour, in an ocean red with blood and foam.

Figure 24 "Fumi" on its way home with a whale tied to its side.

The unfortunate creature was hauled to the side of the ship and firmly secured. An incision was then made in the abdomen to enable the seawater to cool the carcass down, but even after being towed into the station twelve hours later, it would often register ninety degrees Fahrenheit. If only one whale were in the vicinity it would, when killed, be inflated with compressed air and cast adrift with a marker buoy and beeper, to be retrieved after another had been captured.

**Figure 25 Buoys marking the spot of a whale waiting for pickup by the ship returning to the station later that day.**

Sometimes the whale would plunge into the abysmal depths, pulling the rope under the ship causing her to keel over at a dangerous angle. The engines would then be shut down, and everyone waited anxiously, hoping the rope would not become entangled in the propeller. Later in the day, the huge creatures, having been well lashed to the ship, presented a rather hideous appearance; the mass of bloodied intestines, with the huge tongue weighing about two tons, lolling out of a cavernous mouth.

The Fumi, made of iron, sat very low in the water, its deck being only some ten to twelve inches above the water line. The only raised portion was the raised bow and bridge structure. One night, about dark, we were steaming through a placid ocean, in the path of the setting sun, when a school of killer whales suddenly appeared, intent on partaking of a delectable meal of whale tongue.

I was standing near the rail right in their path when the leader came rushing toward me. It seemed certain that he would come on deck without fail. His huge jaws were opened wide revealing rows of razor-sharp teeth, as he grabbed a big slice of the tongue, skillfully swerving at right angles to the boat and off to the rear. Another followed it and yet another until nine of the creatures had taken their share of the tongue. They circled far away from the ship and once again returned until not a vestige was left.

I stood there not three feet away from their gaping jaws, feeling fascinated and yet utterly petrified and helpless. I did, however, grab my movie camera, which I carried at all times, only to find afterwards that there was no more film left. It had been used to film the harpooning of the whales earlier in the day. This all happened so quickly that I had no time to check the camera. I regretted everafter not having been able to film the incident, knowing full well that the opportunity might never arise again. Some of the whales showed evidence of shark attacks. Many schools of porpoises and tuna were commonly seen, the former cavorting around the ship for two hours at a time.

On arrival at the station, if still dark, the whales were secured by a hawser to the shore, and allowed to sink to the bottom of the harbour. This enhanced the cooling of the carcass until the work of flensing (removing the outer layer of blubber or fat) and cutting up of the meat could begin. They were then hauled by a steam-operated winch onto the flensing deck. This was a wooden-raft-like structure raised a few inches above a concrete underlay, slanting toward the shoreline for drainage. Steel cables were used to haul up the carcasses.

Figure 26 Whales being cut up on the flensing deck at Williamsport.

Following this, men or flensers, trained especially for the work, wearing spiked boots to prevent slipping, climbed onto the carcass and began making lengthwise incisions, down to the fat, from the mouth to the tail. These were made in parallel form about three feet apart, following with a large hook attached to the steel cable on the winch, which was inserted at one end of the slice. It was then pulled off in large strips, up a ramp, where others of the gang, cut it into smaller portions feeding it to the digesters. These were rendering tanks heated by steam that extracted the oil from the blubber layer.

Figure 27 Whale on the flensing deck.

The product was then tested for viscosity and purity and stored in large oil-type tanks for later shipment. Meanwhile the meat was cut into blocks weighing about one hundred pounds. Later these in turn were cut into smaller two-pound portions, put into cartons, and stored until shipped in freezers at minus twenty degrees Fahrenheit. The corrugated under-part was made into bacon, and the liver, kidneys, and other organs were packed separately, and viewed as a great delicacy by the Japanese. The immense skeleton was towed up the rendering ramp, with other residue and made into bone-meal fertilizer. Most of the product was shipped to Norway and Japan in refrigerated boats, which called at the station periodically. The last cargo, mostly of meat, would leave on a Japanese ship in late October or early November, an occasion that called for a gala celebration.

The Health of Animals staff, and that of the Fisheries, was invited on board to partake of a feast fit for a king. The fare included shrimp cocktail, small pieces of whale meat (raw), beef cooked on a brassier right on the table, side dishes of whale meat dipped in soya sauce, and a variety of vegetables. Saki wines and Japanese scotch were in good supply, and the festivities went well into the following morning.

Being satiated with all the excellent food and drink, I retired for a good night's sleep, conscious of the fact that I would not have to get up at six o'clock to conduct an inspection of processed whale products. Leaving the wharf to the playing of Auld Lang Syne and Japanese music, the ship left harbour at noon the following day, taking all of their countrymen, except E. Terrada, who later went to St. John's. I grew to love and respect these kindly people who felt that anything we asked of them was not too much.

The anatomical structure of whales certainly supports the theory that this huge, gentle creature once lived on land and has a high degree of intelligence. Stories of their attacking small whaling boats are in my view totally without foundation. One incident, which I felt, was due to the inquisitiveness of the whale, rather than any vicious intention on its part, happened shortly before we finally left Williamsport.

Four young people working on the station visited a settlement called Harbour Deep, some twelve miles down the coast. They used a fourteen-foot outboard motorboat and on returning at dusk, were pursued by two whales which repeatedly dove under their boat, at times almost capsizing it. They eventually eluded the mammals when nearing the harbour's mouth, and were in a state of great agitation on arrival. I concluded that the creatures were attracted by the noise of the motor, and were merely investigating it.

I was rather relieved when the Canadian government decided to prohibit the hunting of these hapless creatures. They were undoubtedly in danger of extinction and hunting from factory ships helped, in large measure, to bring this about. However, in a country such as Japan, where farming is very limited and the population great, it may be necessary to permit limited harvesting. These people have depended on this source of protein for many centuries, and there is no doubt they make good use of every ounce of the animal.

# CHAPTER XVIII - THE SEAL HUNT

In contrast with the killing of whales, the cessation of which I feel was a wise and necessary move on the part of the Canadian Government, I would be remiss if I did not make mention of the controversy surrounding the seal hunt. In Newfoundland the sealing captains of forty years ago, and indeed for a hundred years before, were the aristocrats of the fishermen. They were a fine staunch breed of men trained in the hardest of schools for great self-reliance, resourcefulness, and skill in the handling of ships and men.

As a young man, my imagination was fired with tales of hardship and heroism endured by these Vikings of the ice on the annual seal hunt. Sturdy vessels of the fleet would plough their way into St. Anthony Harbour late in March or April to take on supplies and water. Two, I remember well, were the Neptune and Imogine, with hulls eighteen inches thick, sheathed with "greenhart" to help batter the thick ice floes. The bows were double stemmed and covered with a broad band of iron, and the space between the two stems were solid with the choicest of hardwoods. The vessels were baroque, rigged with auxiliary steam, or rather one should say a steamer with auxiliary sails.

**Figure 28 The sealing ship "Arctic Endeavour."**

Masters of the watches were called scunners whose duty was to climb high into the forebarrel on the foremast and scun the ship, that is to say, find a way through the ice floes. The killing of seals, be they whitecoats babies (bedlamers) or adults, did not at any time convey to my mind a sense of inhuman cruelty, perpetrated by so-called ruthless savages, as depicted by modern-day opponents who resign it as a slaughter of the innocent. The great seal herds are still quite abundant, and the hunt provides a welcome supplement, both of food and money, to a population in which unemployment at that time of year could well reach thirty percent. Aside from this factor, seal herd control is a very important and vital necessity. If not hunted, they could well decimate the fish population to a point where commercial fishing would be considered uneconomical.

My only objection, if any, centers around the extravagant waste of an important source of protein in the form of carcasses left on the icefloes. It would require a great deal of organization, time and money to retrieve these carcasses, and also induce the public at large to accept seal meat as a staple in the diet. The taking of baby seals undoubtedly means the difference between a profitable and worthless voyage. Their skins of soft white fur provide many end products such as fur coats and slippers for the fashion world. Their fat not acquiring the fishy taste yet can be rendered and made into food products. Being fairly immobile, they are easily captured, a great advantage to men having to operate on slippery moving ice pans. Being directly involved in the slaughter of animals for several years, I see no difference in the slaughtering of lambs, calves, or young pigs to provide delicious chops, cutlets, or in the case of seals, flippers for meat dinners. The whole concept is, I must admit, distasteful to many people, but what other alternative is there? The crux lies in carrying out the quickest method of dispatching the poor creatures in the most humane manner possible.

We must not let sentiment and emotion, evoked by the rather forlorn-looking helpless whitecoats, blind us to the fact that until ocean farming regarding seals, can be made economically worthwhile, the present method of taking the most easily accessible member of the seal family, seems to be the only practical one. Those who are most critical should take a more reasonable approach to find ways and means of harvesting seals of all ages within reason. It is a heritage of which Newfoundlanders are proud, the heroism and tragedy being interwoven in the long history of a courageous and resourceful people.

With the cessation of whaling, the closing of W.1. at Williamsport was inevitable. It was of great relief to my wife, stuck with five teenagers four months of each summer. I returned to the Regional Office in Moncton, filling in here and there for veterinarians away on furlough. In 1970, I assumed the duties of Veterinarian-in-Charge of the Northern Meat Packers in Campbellton, a small town situated on the New Brunswick-Quebec border.

The plant was owned and operated by a Mr. Pierre Bourgoin with an able foreman Gaston Avril. The Restigouche Abattoir Company had operated a custom slaughtering business on the site for a few years, but did not process the meat products. Pierre or Pete, as I came to address him, decided to expand into the processing and marketing of meats under government inspection, and cooperated in bringing the plant up to acceptable standards.

He invested a great deal of money, eventually employing about one hundred people, but, as the banks would say "over extended" himself. In spite of having built up a viable business pouring thousands of dollars into the economy of the small city, his credit was cut off, forcing him to close. Only one familiar with the cost of expensive stainless-steel equipment demanded by authorities in a government-inspected establishment, can fully realize the situation. Human fiber can only stand so much strain without financial backing, and in this case it snapped. It is rather ironic that millions of taxpayer's dollars can be found to support idle men and women, who could have been gainfully employed had a little more resourcefulness been given to finding ways and means of supporting an established business.

The seventies brought about many changes in our family life. Peter and Ralph secured jobs with the Canadian National Railway, and married. Elizabeth (Libby) worked as a medical secretary in Thunder Bay, Ontario, and subsequently graduated in nursing while raising a family. Daphne, one of the twins, graduated from the Saint John School of Nursing in New Brunswick, later marrying and moving to Edmonton, Alberta. David, her twin, entered Mount Allison University at Sackville, New Brunswick. In 1979, he earned a Bachelor of Music Degree and then attended the Royal Conservatory of Music at Toronto University in the opera division to further his studies in voice.

# CHAPTER XIX - MIGUASHA LODGE

We invested in a business known as Miguasha Lodge in Quebec, at the Quebec terminus of the Miguasha-Dalhousie ferry, operating in the summer on the Bay of Chaleur. Much of the business was derived from the New Brunswick side, where the sale of beer and spirits was prohibited on Sundays. However, in 1977, the Government of Quebec decided to allow the sale of beer by the case from small grocery stores on Saturday nights and Sundays, which dealt an almost lethal blow to small hotels. Since it could be obtained in bulk at a lower price than that charged by hotels, many of the public purchased it by the case and found a sunny enclave on the nearby beaches to indulge, instead of patronizing our type of establishment. Of course it was successful for the small grocery stores or depanieurs. It definitely made our business much more difficult to promote. A new strategy had to be worked out countering this threat.

Romance, especially with the environment, plays a great part in determining the reason for certain moods. The industrialist sees a forest of virgin timber as a way to acquire material gains. The environmentalist envisions an area where people can escape the pressures of modern living and enjoy the fundamental urge to find the life God intended. Ordinary citizens, as exhibited in modern society, have still not, most fortunately, accepted the dog-eat-dog attitude.

So it was, that Miguasha Lodge was situated in an idyllic environment. The view overlooked the beautiful Bay of Chaleur with the cry of loons echoing in the early morning, in the eerie stillness, and the myriad of lights reflecting Dalhousie in its waters at night. A beautiful setting but like everything else, it had to make a dollar to exist. Everything went well until the bureaucracy of politics and politicians applied a blanket law to all operations which, by their influence, might bring a few more dollars or votes.

The political climate was moving quickly and adversely in la belle province. French was spoken, especially in business, although they had agreed to adopt English as their national language during Lord Durham's era. Treaties and promises became obsolete and then in the so-called "new era" everything English was quelled. Thus it was that the influence of radicals in Quebec asserted their authority through legislation to the detriment of the people at large. Granted, many of those who supported them were drawn from populations such as Royal University undergraduates who had never done an honest day's work in their lives, but who knew it all. These were the people who were sent out to advise others how to set up a business.

Prior to purchasing the Lodge, the former owner had operated it as a summer business. Without doubt, it was ideally located but too far removed from a populated area. The discovery of a fossil deposit nearby and its development by the Quebec government did little to encourage activity. It may be presumptuous to say that the business may have been purchased without undue thought. The accounts indicated that it was a viable business and prior to the government of Quebec allowing beer and wine sales from depaniers on weekends, it was a moderately profitable undertaking.

**Figure 29 I was ready to take on this new challenge!**

After the first couple of years, however, it was quite apparent that operating in winter was out of the question. We had installed base electric heaters which only served partially to heat the outer area away from the kitchen, which itself was heated by a large old-fashioned wood-burning stove. We blew in insulation to all of the building, which helped quite a bit during the fall and winter. Let it be said that I was inveigled into the sale by someone who knew the ropes and, who also knew enough not to be absolutely honest in dealings with others. One thing which particularly annoyed and concerned the staff happened when potential customers, driving up in their cars, asked in English, if we spoke French. When the answer was negative, they immediately drove away with a sneer.

On one occasion, my wife thought it would be nice to serve a meal of beef bourgignon for lunch on a cold autumn day. Entering the rough driveway to the Lodge, the container containing this bourgignon tipped over and the contents spilled on the floor of the car. The ingredients had been made at the house and were to be reheated at the Lodge. Feeling quite baffled, we decided to scrape the spilled contents off the rubber floor mat into a clean container. Little did the few clients that showed up for the luncheon realize that they were partaking of, as my wife said, "Sole" food.

The precious owner, who I was told had engineered some rather shady deals around the area, may have falsely represented the true value of Miguasha Lodge. When I inspected the chalets, a rather outdated group of seven cabins she said they were all rented to people from Montreal and other locations. I checked out the only one she advised was open, finding all the furniture meticulously clean and arranged. No clients appeared on that day to enter their rooms or during the following weekend.

After a sudden storm, the rain came pouring into each one. Fearing the worst, I immediately ordered rolls of good roofing and applied it, hoping to repair the leaks. When I informed the seller of the situation, she denied that she had ever known of any leaks. Another time, vandals broke into the cabins at night and threw all the contents over a bank leading to the beach. It was quite obvious that it was a subtle way of persuading me to get rid of the business.

About a year later, interest rates climbed dramatically and although the seller had, in the name of goodwill, loaned me fifteen thousand dollars at ten-percent interest, she insisted that unforeseen circumstances forced her to raise the interest on the loan to twenty-three percent. I concurred it was only a ploy to force me to sell the Lodge back to her for a greatly reduced price.

Other incidents led weight to my suspicion, but only made me more determined to make a go of things. In view of the anticipated client increase due to the opening of the Miguasha Museum, I thought a small restaurant might be a good idea and engaged an architect to draw plans for presentation to the Industrial Development Bank in Rimouski. They were quite impressed. The mortgage on the Lodge had been paid off, and, in my view, no obstacle stood in the way. However, nothing was arranged and no word ever came to me why it was refused. I was later to find out others had some influence working in and around this particular group of people. Eventually an offer to purchase the property was received and I managed to recover my investment, plus a little.

**Figure 30 Sharrie and I with our children, Peter, Ralph, Libby, Daphne, David and Peter's wife Colleen.**

# CHAPTER XX - RETIREMENT

With the Lodge disposed of, and after a long association with the veterinary profession, I decided to retire wholly from that way of life. For obvious reasons, I have held professional ethics throughout, that is to say with the exception of the burying of the dogs ashes mentioned earlier. An old saying states "You can't make a silk purse out of a sow's ear" and although I don't want to demean any particular veterinarian, it would have been better if some individuals had never been allowed to represent the profession.

We were taught that the aim of our work was to protect the food supply of the country, not to present ourselves as glorified babysitters to the small animal population, as seems to be the case with many of our recent graduates. The main objective seems to be, spare no scruples, charging exorbitant fees to the point of absurdity. I realize this is a national and international tendency, but one which must be checked. The tendency to become bigger and more elaborate, just like large malls, to the detriment of the small operator, has become the norm for a good number of our colleagues. The old-time family veterinarian is rapidly becoming a thing of the past, though I wonder if the replacement is an improved alternative. From all reports, this is also evidenced in family medicine, but in the former, the patient unfortunately has no recourse against the inviolate diagnosis of the veterinarian doctor.

**Figure 31 Sharrie and I enjoying our role as "Snowbirds" in Florida.**

    A few years ago, we purchased a modest home in Florida, annually enjoying six months away from the cold north. Our son, David, having shown a keen interest in opera, his favourite musician being Mozart, decided to pursue this channel of endeavor. David with Jenny Harrison, his wife, opened The Boston Children's Opera in the U.S.A. This has met with outstanding success. My wife and I participated in two operas. My adeptness at playing the harmonica served to enhance the native music. My wife, however, on these occasions, as their page-turner, became so engrossed on the stage, she forgot to turn the pages. One glare from David soon corrected this tendency, and the loud applause from the audience supported our contention that the opera had full support from those present. These wonderful events for a grandfather of eighty-eight years, and my wife of lesser years, is indeed a compliment! We might just put Laurel and Hardy to shame yet! What is now around the corner of life for us, we have yet to see. Nothing would surprise me now!

*A Newfoundland Son*

*Nathan Budgell, DVM*

# AFTERWARD

Since my book's finish, Peter, my eldest son has now retired from the C.N.R. and resides in Moncton, New Brunswick with his family. He and his wife, Colleen, have started a business making beautiful hand-painted chalk ware figurines. Ralph, now also retired from the C.N.R., with his wife Leigh, will run their campground and RV park in beautiful Blue River, British Columbia, while residing in Jasper, Alberta during the winter months. Libby lives in Cornwall, Ontario with her family. She is nursing and helping her husband, Steve in his chiropractic business. David and Jenni are doing well with their Children's Opera in Boston, Massachusetts. Daphne and her family live in Florida where she continues nursing and her husband, Kevin, teaches physical education. My wife Sharrie and I are still spending the winter months in Florida and the summer months visiting our children and their families in Canada.

Figure 32 Fishing for "Moby" in Blue River, British Columbia.

# ABOUT THE AUTHOR

Nathan McKinley Budgell was born in Brown's Cove, Newfoundland on April 23, 1912. He grew up in an orphanage in St. Anthony and was educated in England, graduating with distinction from Chadacre Agricultural Institute in 1930. After working on projects for the Grenfell Association in Newfoundland and Labrador, he went on to receive his Doctor of Veterinarian Medicine in 1939 at Toronto University of Guelph, Ontario. Discharged from the army in 1945, he met and married Florence (Sharrie) Hull with whom he has five children. He lived and worked in the near north, survived the Great Depression and participated in World War II. Throughout his life he maintained a veterinarian practice while trying his hand at a number of other enterprises in various provinces. With Sharrie, he spends the winter in Florida and the summer in Canada remembering a very full life.

Printed in the USA
CPSIA information can be obtained
at www.ICGtesting.com
LVHW090047201223
766959LV00047B/515